BEHIND
DOOR
B

BEHIND DOOR B

a memoir

Julia Askew

Espirit Libre Books

First published in Great Britain in 2023 by Espirit Libre Books

Copyright © 2023 by Julia Askew
Formatted by The Amethyst Angel
Cover Image © 2023 by Lucja Fratczak-Kay

ISBN: 979 838 68 7382 0

ACKNOWLEDGMENTS

Essentially, like a lot of memoirs, I wrote this for myself, not certain if I wanted anyone else to read it, but finally I thought that it may as well see the light of day, publish and be damned. When something takes over 20 years to be written, specific acknowledgements are tricky, but here goes;

My husband Mike has always been encouraging, proof reading for me and believing that it would all come to fruition, so thank you to him for supporting my long hours at the computer.

To my wonderful children, you are the reason I have worked so hard over the years to be whole and okay with who I am, so that I could be present in your lives. Writing this memoir has been all about that. You may not read this yet, but I hope you will be ready to read my story one day and will be proud of me.

To all the special women in my life, I will never underestimate the power of strong female friendships, so sadly lacking in this memoir. Thank you for being there, for understanding and for listening, you all know who you are.

Michelle Gordon of Amethyst Angel has me given invaluable help in the final stages of getting the book into print and over the line. Self-publishing is not for the faint hearted and I could not have done it without her help and support.

It is far easier than you might imagine to find yourself in a relationship where you do not feel safe. Where the person who says they love you also bullies you, controls you, hurts you. That toxic and confusing mix of love and hurt can mean that you stay for years, in the shadows, hidden from everyone.

This book is for everyone hiding in the shadows. I hope with all my heart that you can find the strength to come out into the light, tell someone, get help and find a safer future.

PROLOGUE

Warning, this book is written in the first person. Some people don't like books that are written this way because you never get to find out what other people in the story are thinking, so potentially, it's all a bit one dimensional or me me me, but I'm not going to apologise for that, because this is a memoir of a very hard and pivotal time in my life.

It covers 6 years in the 1980s. Not the best 6 years of my life insofar as that would not be much of a story; another contented day, had a lovely time, nothing much happened. Probably because of the 6 years in question, I now quite like the mundane and boring, the calm and the quiet. These 6 years do not involve exotic locations, unless you count Kingston-upon-Hull and Darlington, which to a southerner like me were pretty exotic at the time.

Spoiler alert, obviously, I had not intended to become a battered wife (a wonderfully colourful expression of the time, which now just makes me think of a nice bit of haddock). I say obviously, because in most womens' eyes it is not high on their top ten list of life's ambitions. Becoming a battered wife was about as far from my imagination as becoming the Queen of England, which at the time, as Diana had just snatched the heir to the throne from under my very nose, was even more unlikely.

This all took place 40 years ago, 1982 through to 1988. I haven't changed the names of the main characters in this story, but I have changed or left out the names of some of the minor characters.

Time does dull memories and so there is some artistic licence, but the main events are as clear in my mind now as they were the day they happened. Even if no one ever does me the honour of reading and liking my story, writing it is cathartic (for me at least). It's ugly, it's snotty and horrible in places, and in other places occasionally funny and uplifting and all those other things that a messy life can be.

The typical question - What would you change about your life if you could? - drives me crazy, because I would probably rewrite a lot of the 6 years in question, but I will never have the option to change what happened, only do what we all do when bad things happen, and that is live with it. I have not written this because I want people to feel sorry for me, within these pages are my nistakes and achievements, and in reading it I hope you will see how easy it is to take the wrong road for the right reasons and just have to keep on going with all that it entails. I started writing it down over 20 years ago on the advice of a therapist, but it has taken me until nearly 40 years later, to finish it and be brave enough to publish and be damned!

> *"At the end of the day, we can endure much more than we think we can."*
> *Frieda Kahlo*

CHAPTER ONE

Coming Home

One very bright August day in 1982, I decamped into the arrivals lounge of Gatwick airport, no longer the wrong side of the Atlantic, and the right side of a very short first marriage to a nice, but very boring American guy called Tom. I was full of hope for a brighter and happier and more interesting future, leaving my past mistakes behind me. Of course, this particular state of mind denied my very nature, but more of that later.

I was a well brought up middle-class, horse-riding girl from rural middle England, who said grass with an extra "r". So how did I end up living in a two up two down terraced house in the dark wind-swept northeast of England, married to a working-class bloke, who sounded like Sting? I don't mean to be derogatory about the Northeast, the dark wind-swept bit is for dramatic effect, think of Catherine and Heathcliff and then forget them as this story bears no resemblance to their story and there are no moors involved.

John (main protagonist and afore-mentioned husband) was 'working class', it was how he described himself and he was proud of it. He kept racing pigeons, spent a lot of time in the pub when it was open, which was not all the time in those days luckily. He left the extra "r" out of grass and his favourite expression was 'Those were the days when men were men and woman knew where the ground was', after which he would always laugh, and I would laugh too, because I thought he was being ironic and sadly I have to admit to finding this endearing at the beginning of our relationship.

What was my excuse? He was handsome, highly intelligent, charming and witty, he had what you would call charisma in spades. He was also a very gifted Special Education teacher and as he had what I considered to be a very hard and worthy job, I did put him onto something of a pedestal. But he was not the perfect human you might imagine from my description, as he had a penchant for violence, which he meted out throughout our relationship in a fairly arbitrary way.

John was my second husband, the first being the nice, affable but boring American boy I fled from, having married him in an unguarded moment of stupidity. The ease with which I did stupid things was a force to be reckoned with as I ploughed disastrously though my late teens and twenties and into the 1980s. I was without thought or purpose, often jobless, often without a home of my own and often friendless. Or to be more specific, I did have jobs, just crap ones, I did have places to live, just crummy ones and I did have friends, just not good ones. In those 6 years I had too many of the first two and not enough of the last. And to make it all just about perfect, I had a second husband who turned out to be far worse than the first.

Not what anyone would choose for themselves, I hear you say, but making wrong decisions was my forte. You know the ones; behind door A is health, wealth and happiness and Mr or Mrs Right. Behind door B hides despair, Mr or Mrs couldn't be more wrong for you and for good measure, a man-eating tiger, which hasn't been fed for a week. (I don't mean to give tigers a bad press you understand, they have a hard enough time of it from us humans, so that there are not nearly enough of them to make much impact on the human population by making us a snack, but they suit my analogy so there you go).

So, when the time came to choose between metaphorical door A or door B, I would rush blindly through door B, emerging a week, a month or in this case 6 years later, with my right leg badly chewed by the starving tiger, but otherwise pretty much back where I started. Progress: none, lessons learnt: plenty, but I was young and optimistic, and I forgot the lessons pretty quickly. Being an optimist, expecting good outcomes, trusting people, assuming it would all work out, has not always served me (understatement no. 1). I believed that no matter what, everything would work out and be OK, all I had to do was hang on in there, bide my time and as if by magic, everything wrong would right itself, the sun would come out tomorrow, just you wait and see (cue song). When I run back over the thought processes leading to the decision to open door B, I would find that in fact there hadn't been very many thoughts to speak of, pure instinct and gut reactions led me there, and my instincts and gut reactions were overall pretty poor. So, take one very naïve, misguided and perhaps stupid young woman and get on with the story.

After my first marriage ended, I flew home from the States, two years older, but you've guessed it, no wiser in any way. I had never really got on with the USA, I didn't fit in there, I missed the UK and apart from my husband, Tom, my US family were not particularly friendly to me. Had I given it a chance? You bet your bottom dollar I had!

In my defence, there were things about the States I did like. Pistachio ice cream, BLTs, Mac and Cheese from a packet, - as yet all undiscovered in the culinary time warp that was Britain at the time (although I am not sure they made up for me missing British cheddar and bacon). I also liked the state of Maine – beautiful, New England in the fall – astonishing, and my husband's best friend – far too tempting for an unhappy woman. But they did not make up for a cockroach infested basement partment in Boston that was freezing in the winter and boiling hot in the summer. I had several dreadful jobs including a coat check girl and a peanut packer (admittedly I only lasted a day at that), Burger King (managed a whole month, but the burns got too much), and a photocopier operator, all this in spite of my very lofty British University education. I did eventually get a receptionist job at an IT company that I quite enjoyed as they liked my English accent

Speaking of which, having a fairly posh English accent in Irish Boston during the Northern Ireland troubles didn't do me any favours either when it came to job hunting. Did I mention the abysmal TV as the icing on the cake? Although that might have been having a husband who was asleep by 9.30 every evening,

I was only 23 and I felt like my life was over. And just to rub salt in the wound, they could not say my name properly which is spelt Julia and is pronounced Jew-lee-a, three very clear syllables. They said Jul(rhymes with Gull)-ya, with the 2 syllables mashed together with the wrong vowel in the middle, I found it upsetting, I was always on the back foot, defensive and unrooted.

So finally, with more thought than I had given to my arrival, I packed up a rented station wagon, left a note on the mantelpiece saying 'it was all me, not you, please move on in your life, so sorry, etc.,' and drove from Boston all the way down Route 95 to Tampa Bay, Florida where my Aunt lived, to meet up with my mum and dad (who were there visiting) and fly home. They were rather pleased with my decision and did nothing to dissuade me. I don't think they liked Tom very much to be honest. I felt bad about the note, but this was cancelled out by the huge relief of being home again.

I heard years later that Tom had been in a bad car accident and had ended up in a wheelchair. I felt responsible as only those prone to guilt can. Rationalising that I had nothing to do with it was not much help. My leaving changed the course of his life and ultimately his destiny. Unless it was his destiny for me to leave? Isn't karma complicated.

I was returning to my parents who were ensconced, for the most part unhappily, in leafy Oxfordshire. Whilst in Florida and on the long flight home they had been solicitous and gave freely of their opinions on what I did wrong, what he did wrong, and what I should do now. I had no idea what I wanted to do. I filed their wise words under 'crap advice from parents who don't understand me', so maintaining my good relationship with them.

I really did have absolutely no idea what I wanted to do, except get a divorce and have some fun. I was only twenty-three, bright (forget what I said before), a graduate of a good university, attractive and with no debts or ties whatsoever. Any other girl in her right mind would have found a reasonable office/graduate job in London, a flat with some other like-minded girls and proceeded to have that good time, find a man, or woman depending on what rocked her boat, or enjoyed a procession of men or women, depending on how good a time she wanted.

This would have resulted in a completely different story, which would have probably been a bestseller, the opportunity for single females hunting for the right partner and the ensuing angst and happy ending being very popular in the bookshops. I did something entirely different. Door B had my name on it again, the man-eating tiger was still a bit hungry. My powers of reasoning and decision-making kicked in just one minute too late.

This one-minute too late was after my ex-boyfriend Chris arrived (rather romantically I thought; see where I went wrong?) on my parent's doorstep two hours after I had arrived home from the airport. I never did find out how he knew I was back; I like to think it was telepathy.

It went a little like this:

Opening the door, "Hi, you," he smiled, "One down, six to go, Julia."

"I shall never marry again," I declared emphatically.

"That," he paused dramatically, "remains to be seen. Come down the White Horse."

Chris ambled into the kitchen, looking like he did it regularly, which one boyfriend and one husband ago he had done. It was just 15 months since I had seen him, drunk at my wedding, trying to seduce my college friends, whilst still drunkenly declaring that it should have been him to my brothers in the toilets. The easy familiarity we had seeped back between us. He slumped at the pine farmhouse table.

"I have come to take your daughter down the pub,

now she has seen sense and returned to the fold," he said to my mum and dad.

I was jet lagged and only wanted a bath and my bed. But I was flattered that he had come to see me so soon after my return, and the thought of a proper pint of bitter in a lovely English county pub, the opportunity to indulge in a big dose of mutual piss-taking and haranguing, won the day.

"Mummy, Daddy, I'll see you later," I said before they had a chance to tell me that they hadn't seen much of me for the last two years and would Chris like to stay for something to eat. I left them to finish their unpacking, having abandoned mine all over the spare bedroom and we went outside to get into Chris' car. It was his usual heap of rust, though mechanically sound and tinkered with to go very fast. His cars always looked like they were one day from going to the scrapyard. This one was orange, the make and model a well-kept secret.

"Great car this!" he said enthusiastically, "Got the engine just right, goes like a dream."

"Doesn't look like one though, looks like a nightmare."

"You'll see, get in."

As the engine burst into life and settled into the dull hum of mechanical perfection, Chris turned to me before we drove off.

"My Jules, back. I mean I knew it would happen, I didn't think it would be quite so soon though, I had you down for another year at least, reduce the embarrassment factor."

"I am no longer *your* Jules, Chris, I am not embarrassed and what do you mean you knew it would happen?"

"You're too English to be happy over there, and that plonker you married, well enough said."

"Look, Mr Expert on Married Life, Tom was not a plonker he was just American, and they are sweeping generalisations. It is much more complicated than that, anyway I don't want to discuss it just now, let's go to the pub please," I pleaded, "I'd love a proper pint."

Fifteen minutes later, we were sitting in the White Horse pub garden. It was one of those perfect balmy August evenings; the sun was very low, making all the windows in the Cotswold stone houses on the opposite side of the valley shine like liquid gold. It was a lovely pub, ivy covered, nestling opposite the village green of the small Cotswold village.

In the winter it was cosy with an open fire, bare limestone brick walls and highly polished horse brasses twinkling in the firelight, with the ubiquitous tatty old farmer or two holding sway at the bar. I know there used to be thousands of pubs like it across rural Britain, but I loved this one, it was quintessential and perfect. Limestone houses and cottages of all shapes and sizes rose up around the pub and green. A small stream ran through the green into a millpond and then on who knows where. A ford crossed it from the road coming down the hill. I had ridden out this way many times in the past; the horses had loved wading in the shallow water, pawing at the mud.

I had never owned the ponies or horses I rode; I had ridden for free in return for helping out at the riding stables. However, whenever small girls' envious eyes had turned on me as I rode the ponies in the ford or some other idyllic spot, I would make believe and make them believe that this was my own beloved Comet or Silver, ready to go home to his stable and field behind my house.

"Penny for them," Chris said as he sat opposite me and deposited two pints of Wadworths 6X onto the table.

"I was just remembering coming here with the ponies from the stables, they loved wading in the water."

"Not much chance to ride in Boston, then?" he asked.

"Not in this kind of setting. No, I have missed it."

"Have you missed me?" he asked, turning the conversation to himself as only he could do.

"Not specifically," I offered.

"Generally, then?" he asked hopefully.

I satisfied him with a "Yes, along with real sausages, bacon and cheese, fish and chips, Branston pickle, HP sauce, Doctor Who, Blakes Seven, and the Queen's English."

"A lot then."

"So, Chris, what have you been up to for the last two years? Do tell, and it had better be interesting," I prompted.

"More drinks first, then I will spill the beans."

So, while we sat in the pub chewing the fat and

atching up, I will fill in a little background on why someone who was not my boyfriend (anymore) should turn up on my doorstep hours after my return to the UK and then drag me off to the pub.

Chris was my second ever boyfriend. I met him at school. He wasn't the boy that I lost my virginity to, but he was the first boy I had an orgasm with, which I like to think is probably more important. I wish he had been both, but you can't change that.

We were at school together in what used to be called the upper six, I was 17, and he was 18, repeating his second year after screwing up his A levels the year before. He was very funny, intelligent with a capital I; he could draw and paint amazing pictures and play the piano like a pro. He wasn't handsome, he was striking, with incredibly bright blue eyes and long thick black curly hair. Cocky and sure of himself on the outside, soft and vulnerable on the inside as I later found out. He was in the more cerebral group, geeks as they would be known today. Physics and Chemistry and Maths were his main subjects, but he was in the rugby team too. He listened to Emerson, Lake and Palmer, Pink Crimson and Yes on the sixth form record player when it was the geeks turn to pick the records.

I only had one real friend in school – Janet. I was into horse-riding exclusively and had been since I was 11, and so was Janet. I didn't do Physics or Chemistry or Maths, having been encouraged by my parents to focus on more 'female' subjects, but I was fascinated with

Chris, because he was so different to everyone else than I knew. I hatched a plan to snare my man. Myself and my brothers had somehow convinced my parents that we needed to have a small New Year's Eve party to see out 1975. God knows how, it seems inconceivable even now, but we had, and it happened. Very bravely and casually I wandered over to Chris at school and invited him, well it was a bit of a blanket invitation to all the geeks, although I only wanted him to come.

There I was at the party, it got to 11 o'clock and I just thought; he's not coming, he's not coming. And then suddenly there he was, stood in front of me in a gorilla mask with his long black greatcoat on, a long knitted colourful scarf wrapped around his neck and a bowler hat on his head. All of these were references of the time, the bowler hat was a nod to the film *Clockwork Orange*, the scarf a reference to Dr Who and Chris Baker who he had an uncanny resemblance to funnily enough. The gorilla mask, well I don't think that was a reference to anything other than shock factor, and once he took it off, I was just thrilled that he was there and couldn't help the smile that wouldn't leave my face. He had a smile to match, too. I ignored my other guests for the rest of the evening. At midnight, we were still smiling and dancing our hearts out to *Bohemian Rhapsody*, which had just become number one for the first time around. He said very nonchalantly as he left, "Do you fancy a drink next week?"

Well, I think I might have said, well, in fact I know I

said "Yes, yes, I would really like to do that."

And that was the start of nine glorious, wonderful, love-filled months during which we both had to revise for and then sit our A levels to get into university, and then enjoy the long hot summer of 1976, before going off to our respective universities in October. Our universities turned out to be only 40 miles apart. 'That will work,' I thought at the time. How silly in love I was.

During that summer we grabbed our moments where we could, mostly in our cars, he had a mini, I had a beat-up Triumph Herald. Passing my driving test the previous summer had opened up a whole new world to me. As it progressed into summer and our A levels were behind us, we spent many an evening driving out to country pubs or finding quiet little lanes with access to wheat fields. I want to say 'corn fields' because it sounds better, but they were wheat fields. We had mats, blankets and cushions in our cars, and we would lay down our mats and cushions and open cans of cider and we would drink, talk, laugh, bonk (still one of my favourite words for the act of sex), filling our free hours with each other. We would sometimes hang out with other friends in various country pubs, but that summer was ours, and ours alone, or so we thought. We would lie back and look up at the sky. One of our favourite fields was on the flight path of a nearby airfield. Lots of planes used to fly over the top of us and we would wave thinking they couldn't possibly see us naked in this wheat field because the wheat never grew so high as it did in 1976.

He worked on a farm, and got strong and brown. I worked as a lock keeper's assistant on the Thames and got strong and brown. It was a great job as due to the water shortage that year I only had to operate the lock once an hour, the rest of the time I sat in the Lock Keeper's hut out of the sun and read all the three *Lord of the Rings* books back-to-back. I wore a bikini to work! We were young, fit and gorgeous, it was, after all the legendary summer of '76 – since gone down in history, and for always in my memory because I spent most of it with Chris.

Chris is not the central character of my story, but he began it, and he wove in and out of it and is an incredibly important part of it to me. When we both went off to our prospective universities at the end of the legendary summer of '76, it turned out not to be as I had imagined. Even though they were only 40 miles apart, we hadn't taken our cars and also we had no way of easily communicating with each other, trying to rely on payphones and the odd letter, so we very quickly drifted apart in the first two terms of Uni, making new friends, having new adventures, studying a bit. I was brutally home sick for the first term and missed Chris so much, but he seemed to be doing OK without me and so our separation began. We both hurt each other and interestingly, in the process, we found new loves and different paths.

Six years down the line from 1976 as I flew back in

from the States, we were still friends, although we had been encouraged by our new partners to limit contact. There was limited acrimony too, although sometimes in the early days of our grown-up lives I had missed him so much it hurt, we had both accepted that it couldn't be helped and that we had to move on. We were still affectionate and drawn to each other, which is what led to my next Door B moment.

Back to 1982 and the White Horse, "I'm still seeing Morgan you know," he said very matter-of-factly as he set the beers down carefully. I looked at him but said nothing, Morgan was the new relationship I just mentioned, not so new at that point, five years down the line, it seemed far too permanent for my liking.

"She's living back with her parents in the Rhondda now, her dad's really ill. I see her a couple of times a month, it's a bloody long drive from Hull, which is where I happen to live right now."

"I'm surprised you bother," I said blithely.

He looked stunned. "I couldn't leave Morgan, she loves me, and we've been through a lot together."

I noticed that he did not say that he loved her. I pulled this thought into myself as dark unreasonable jealousy swept through every cell in my body. I hated Morgan; I had only met her once and decided she was far too beautiful and self-assured. Plus, she had been able to drink an unlimited quantity of Brains SA, a strong bitter particular to South Wales. This proved to be one of her more admirable qualities in Chris' eyes. He was my Chris even if it hadn't worked out. Even if we had gone off with other people at university, even if I had got married and gone to America. Chris and I had gone to school together, he had drawn me in the nude, like the scene in *Titanic* (minus the massive jewel). Things like that were important.

The subject of Morgan was dropped, to our mutual relief, and as the evening progressed, more beer was bought. Chris amused me with tales of what my old school mates were up to. The two people voted most likely never to get laid had married each other. I laughed so much tears ran down my face.

Chris laughed back, "Well at least they've managed to stay married which is more than you've done." He leant forward and whispered conspiratorially to me, "I knew you wouldn't last, nice wedding though."

"Well thanks for telling me," I countered. "Just think of all the marvellous things I could have achieved in the last year and a half instead of being in exile in Boston."

He was right about the wedding, it had been nice, but it had been all downhill from there. I had one last attempt to even out the humiliation score for the evening.

"Anyway, talking of weddings, are you not the one and the same Chris who was overheard in the men's toilets at the Hotel declaring drunkenly to anyone who would listen that it should have been you, that you were the only one who loved and understood me?"

"Very true, you've got me there, but that best man

was really getting my goat, never mind the frilly shirt and bowtie. Hadn't anyone told him what to wear to a normal English wedding? He looked so naff, and he was talking utter bollocks. Bet he feels a right pillock now and wishes that he'd listened to me."

"I think your timing was a little out, hasn't anyone told you, you're supposed to make that kind of speech in the church to stop the poor deluded couple from doing it. Drunken rambling in the toilets at the reception afterwards are not much help, so thanks for nothing."

"I meant it at the time you know."

"What about now?" I queried gently.

"Maybe, yeah maybe," he laughed. "Come on, I'd better get you home."

We made love after the pub; make love/bonk, either way, it was the natural thing to do. It was a warm night. For old times' sake we both declared, drunk and dewy-eyed. Well, I'm not too sure about the dewy-eyed bit, as it was pitch black in the field behind my parent's house. It's only ever that dark in the country. We struggled out of our clothes in time-honoured tradition and lay on the blanket from the boot of his car. It smelt of oil and wasn't quite big enough leaving our legs sticking into the scratchy undergrowth.

What followed was tried and tested, time may have gone by, but it was like putting on an old jumper, erotic in its familiarity, it was comfortable.

"I have to admit, I've missed this," he whispered afterwards.

The tears from my orgasm were still drying on my cheeks, he wiped his thumb across my wet cheek.

"You've missed me too."

"Not you, this."

"So, yank husband number one was crap in the sack."

"All right, I've missed you. Happy now?"

He had come close to the truth with his joshing, but I wasn't going to let him know.

He hugged me fiercely, until my ribs creaked. I wondered why the simple good things in life, like sex with Chris, could be so difficult to have while the crap things fell into my lap no problem.

As we got dressed in the pitch black, he said very casually, "Come up to Hull for a few days, you know, get some space from your folks."

"Chris!" I whispered back, "I have barely seen my parents in two years! But it is appealing. It's so quiet here after Boston. No police sirens."

CHAPTER TWO

The Long Road North

The next day, Chris arrived quite promptly (for him) in the morning. We smiled wryly at each other as we were wearing each other's jeans. In the pitch black in the field behind the house we had just put on whatever clothes came to hand. I was managing okay as his were slightly baggy on me, but he looked hilarious with a rather snugly fitting crotch. My parents were still upstairs so we quickly disappeared into the dining room to swap the jeans over.

"Very embarrassing this morning, I hadn't brought any other clothes. My mum commented on how tight the new fashions were now." He sniggered at me.

I dashed upstairs to say goodbye to my bemused parents, and we headed to the car. In the glare of a perfect summer morning, blue skies, scudding white clouds, a light breeze, birds singing, so English I could have cried, the car revealed itself to be a rusting orange Ford Escort of indeterminate age. I threw my bag cheerfully into the back seat having been told that the boot catch was dodgy. I was a bit unsettled to be able to see the road rushing below me through a small hole in the floor of the passenger footwell. But it did go like a bomb and when sober, Chris was a competent driver, so I tried to put my apprehension to one side and enjoy hurtling through the English countryside to my northern destination.

"So, tell me about Hull," I said casually as we barrelled onto the Fosse Way and headed up through the back roads of Oxfordshire and Leicestershire to meet up with the M1.

"Not much to tell," he began. "Very flat, river through the middle, two rugby league teams, one each side of the river. University, teaching hospital, teacher's training college, lots of girls. Oh, and the Humber bridge which as far as I can tell, no-one uses."

"Sounds interesting, and why exactly are you living there of all places?"

"That's where the Royal Doulton bath making factory is. They are experimenting with designs in plastic baths, using more colours and designs pressed into the plastic, waves, fish, that sort of thing and that my dear is where I come in, I am somewhat of an expert on moulded plastic having done my dissertation on it."

"Who'd have thought of it."

"What are you going to do about getting a job, any

idea where you will live, what you will do?" he enquired casually.

"No, not really, a few options; stay with Mummy and Daddy, cheap but probably not a good idea and I would need a car which I can't afford, head for London, two of my brothers have a house in Southfield near Wimbledon, which sounds quite nice, there's no hurry though, I have a bit of cash to tide me over, something will point me in the right direction, I hope." Always the optimist, I really did believe something would just fall in front of me and I would be a millionaire by 30, or if not at least married to one which would have made my mother very proud.

The miles flew by, the M69, the M1, the A1, the M18, the M180 and finally Hull. After we got onto the M18 traffic dwindled to a few lorries and even fewer cars.

"This road only goes to Hull," was Chris's explanation, "and you only go there if you live there or want to catch a ferry. Suits me, nice quiet personal motorway."

We arrived about mid-day. Hull didn't look particularly like a northern town to me. Perhaps because it was flat, there were no dark satanic mills and brooding moorland vistas. It was all rather pedestrian and genteel and by the sea. I later discovered that there was a strong Georgian influence in the buildings with much of the city being developed in the early 19th century when the port had been booming. There were, of course, the usual grids of street upon street of small terraced houses, with their small yards behind them and alleys running between. I thought scornfully in my privileged middle-class way, about how small they were, never imagining for one minute that one would be my home one day quite soon.

Chris's flat was better than I had expected given the complete shit holes he had lived in at Uni. It looked out over Pearson Park. I was told this was a relatively upmarket place to live in Hull. A biggish square piece of grass with the usual trees, flowerbeds, and paths. Radiating off the Park were avenues of large Georgian or Victorian Houses, many turned into 3 or 4 flats with communal gardens at the back. The area was in fact known as 'The Avenues'.

Chris's flat was the top floor of a 3-story house; the bottom two floors being occupied by the landlady and her sister. Harmless spinsters in their 60s who he said left him alone. His flat had a large sunny living room with a big bay sash window overlooking the park. There was a roomy bedroom at the back with a small bathroom and kitchen off the corridor in-between. It could have been a nice flat, but in time honoured Chris tradition it was a complete pigsty and filthy to boot. Dirty dishes filled the sink to overflowing. The hallway was lined with empty bottles of wine, beer and cider (recycling not being much of a thing then). I may have forgotten to mention that Chris drank prodigiously most days, work and driving permitting. The bed was unmade, covered

1 clothes in various stages of wearing.

He smiled at me wryly as I surveyed the debris. "Heh, ou know me, not known for my domestic skills."

"Too right," I said, determined to sit on my hands ather than clean up his mess.

"So, what do you think?" he said proudly, after he had dragged me around all four rooms ending in the bedroom. He was fairly obviously oblivious to the mess surrounding us.

"Um, very homely, spacious too."

"It's great, first place I have not shared with someone else, it's good to have my own space."

He pulled all the dirty clothes of the bed. "Let's bonk," he said, "then I'll take you down the pub before it closes." Chris was very good at getting his priorities right.

Half an hour later, satisfied and dressed again we strolled down the road towards a pub called The Swiss Cottage. As it was late Saturday lunchtime, Chris was expecting several of his new cohorts to be ensconced, as they were every Saturday lunchtime and most evenings too from what he told me

CHAPTER THREE

Meet the Cast

The Swiss Cottage was a huge modern pub, and with the university and teaching Hospital literally across the road, consequently, it was full of young people spending their grants on the necessities of life, drink and cigarettes. It was busy and buzzing, no-one was eating, the best you could get in a pub in the 80s was a ham or cheese roll from a glass case behind the bar (made fresh that morning if you were lucky) or a packet of crisps or peanuts. In the good old days when smoking inside was almost compulsory, lots of people smoked and consequently, smoker or not (secondary smoking wasn't really a thing), everyone smelt of fags all the time. If you didn't smoke, you might as well do due to the unknown secondary smoking thing. I smoked (although only when I had a drink normally, so was known in the parlance as a 'social smoker', or one of the lucky ones not addicted to nicotine. Chris (who never smoked cigarettes) dragged me straight over to one of the horseshoe shaped booths arranged in back-to-back clusters of 4. The high-backed seats were covered in the ubiquitous standard red velvet with gold trim framed by lots of dark highly varnished wood. In the centre of each booth was a small wooden table with decorative metal legs. This was covered in beer mats in varying stages of decay. The booths were comfortable for 6 people, cosy for 8 people, they guaranteed privacy and gave an unreal sense of intimacy for all of the groups scattered around.

The group we were heading for consisted of 5 people. 4 blokes and a girl. As Chris offered to get a round in and rushed off to the bar to buy beer, him bitter, me lager and lime, it might be best if I just tell you now what I know about these 5 people. It took me about 4 visits to find all of this out, but let me share it now and then I can get on with the rest of the story.

Sean was 25, Irish by name and descent, black hair, blue eyes, big glasses. Looked a bit like Mike Reed off the radio (if you can recall). He had gone to Durham University and was now a supermarket manager for a northern chain of supermarkets that I had never heard of until that moment, but was very big in the northeast, Jacksons, sold later to Sainsburys. He was considered to be doing very well for himself, thank you. He was naturally funny, clever and sort of sexy in a not classically good-looking sort of way and turned out to be a mean dancer when the disco music started. He had a biting and quite vicious wit that he wielded against anyone he considered his inferior. I later found out this was about 99% of the population, and he was probably about right. He rented a flat around the corner from Pearson Park, above a furniture shop.

Gary was a shortish man with overly long hair and a Doobie Brothers moustache, a common look for blokes in the 80s. He had just finished a very messy divorce, involving smashed up houses, restraining orders and a custody battle which he had lost. He was bitter and angry, and a little bit beaten. It was a whole new and fascinating world to me, pathos and pantomime, in the days before the Jeremy Kyle show, it was all going on in Kingston-upon-Hull. He had smashed up his house just before it was repossessed by the bank. "If they think they're going to make a profit out of my misery they've got another thing coming," he ranted at me, assuming that I would be sympathetic. I was appalled but said nothing.

Unsurprisingly, given his penchant for unpredictable behaviour, his ex-wife had taken out a restraining order against him and he had lost the custody battle over his blond haired, blue eyed cherubic son whose tattered picture and teddy bear he carried around and showed to me more or less straight away, and at regular intervals thereafter. I was never entirely sure where he lived, a bedsit I think, grim by the sound of it, I never went there.

It would be years later that I developed what I would describe as post-sympathy for his situation, but I found I had very little at the time, an amicable divorce would probably have resulted in access to his son, I reasoned to myself. I realise now I was being incredibly naïve at the time. To complete the package of misery, he had also lost his job at the supermarket as Sean's sidekick, a bit like Morecambe and Wise, I thought, but with only one funny one. The final battle he was losing was with the drink. He was well on the way to alcoholism, with hands that shook. When he managed to forget his woes for a while and cheered up, he had a nice smile, a wicked twinkle in his eye and I found it easy to like him despite the stories.

The third bloke, Paul, was an art teacher and therefore had the required and acceptable long hair onto his shoulders, tall and lanky, he wore tight black jeans and baggy and holey jumpers or a collarless shirt and waistcoat and looked exactly like he should be playing a guitar in a rock band, very bohemian. He was in his early 30s, had been married once before when he was quite young and had a 15-year-old son. He drank cider and chain smoked and seemed to me to be a romantic dashing figure. He bucked the trend by owning his own house and had a girlfriend that we didn't see very much, who was a little bit younger than him.

And now we come to Dick, the anti-hero of my story. To confuse everyone, although he came to be called John by me and everyone in time, at this point in the story, e was called Dick or Dicky, Richard being his second nd chosen name. Dick was also in his early thirties, ten ears older than me, and he had gone to teacher training ollege with Paul back in the late 60s. Dick worked in a school for children in need of extra help and support with educational and or physical disabilities. He was not overly tall, a few inches shy of 6 feet and was very slim and small boned with an incredible head of thick brown hair, over a pair of small alert green eyes with a distinct oriental slant to them. I found out later that his skinniness was because most of his calories came from drink. He looked a little like Jack Nicholson or Alex Higgins the snooker player, and spoke like a Geordie. I later found out he came from Teesside or Middlesbrough which is just not the same thing as being a Geordie, although to my southern ear at the time he sounded like one.

He kept up the common theme of the group by also drinking like a fish and smoking like a chimney. He also seemed to know an awful lot about nothing at all, spouting facts and figures to support almost any conversation. He too, was divorced from a woman who he had met at teacher training college and been married to for at least 5 years and had a daughter with. The ex-wife was talked about in reverent tones, it seemed she had been a paragon of virtue to put up with him, but she had left him two years before for reasons not specified, and he had not seen his 3-year-old daughter since, as they lived in Lancashire.

Contrary to Gary's situation, he seemed almost proud of his parental detachment, sending off his maintenance every month as if this abdicated him of all further involvement and cleared the slate. I did find out later that this laissez-faire attitude towards his ex-wife and daughter did hide a deep loss that affected him badly.

The fifth person at the table was a girl considerably younger than anyone else there, younger even than me. It turned out she was 19 and a student nurse called Tracey. She was very tall, at least six feet, and very skinny. She was Dick's girlfriend, she lived in the nurse's residence down the road but spent several nights a week at Dick's flat which was also around the corner from the pub.

In our initial meetings I completely failed to see what she saw in Dick or how a man in his thirties could have such a young and pretty girlfriend, as I thought he was ancient. He was also poor and had 'loser' written all over him. I would of course change my mind about all of this, and funnily enough, so would Tracey.

Apart from Paul and Dick who had gone to college together and Gary and Sean who had worked together, I never found out how these two pairs had teamed up, but teamed they were, spending a great deal of time together. These four men were Chris's new friends, and a more motley crew could not have been imagined. They seemed stuck in the seventies, a perpetual student life, living in rented houses, flats or bed-sits without much thought about what the future held for them. The sort of characters that often populated true-life gritty comedies and soaps and even though Chris spoke with a Home Counties accent and had been educated at a public school, he seemed to fit in perfectly.

Being 1982, the pubs were only open until 3pm at lunchtime, can you believe it? So, an hour and a couple of rounds of drinks later, as the others all straggled off to the off licence (called the 'Offy' to the southern uninitiated) to get some drinks (called 'a box' to the southern uninitiated) and retire to someone's flat until the pub re-opened at 6pm, Chris and I decided to retire back to his flat. The jet lag was kicking in and he was promising to cook a corn-beef hash and baked beans for me. I suspected that after being fed I would be expected to clean up which meant cleaning up first in order to get to the sink but fortified with lager and resigned to my fate, I agreed.

It was a nice corn beef hash, and it only took me an hour and several gallons of hot water to make the kitchen habitable afterwards as it included the previous week's dishes and the grime that had managed to accumulate in the six months that Chris had inhabited the flat. We discussed going back out to the pub, but instead went back to bed for a bit, snoozing and having gentle sex until a teatime of hot crumpets and jam followed by slumping in front of the telly with a very large bottle of cider to share between us (mostly drunk by Chris).

After two years of American television which consisted mostly of adverts, baseball and American football and more adverts, I was enthralled enough to remain there for the rest of the evening.

"We know how to have a good time, don't we, Jules?" were some of the only words spoken.

"We do," I replied. "We surely do."

The following day being a Sunday, we slept late and bonked later.

"I don't cook much," was Chris' explanation of the empty cupboards, although this was in the day that takeaways were primarily fish and chips or Chinese food, so I hated to think what he had been living on, nothing good for his arteries that was for sure. After getting up and dressing, leaving him snoozing, I went down to the local corner shop (supermarkets being shut on a Sunday) to buy the necessary bacon, eggs, bread, butter, milk, and baked beans and teabags for our cooked breakfast.

It was going to be a feast to obliterate the memory of brittle over-done non-existent bacon, rubbery scrambled egg, and sweet pancakes and syrup that made up a US breakfast for presidents. And why did I feel the need to do this? OK, I admit it, I am a bit of a walk over, it is the very strong duty gene, caused by being a second child and first daughter, the physiologists among you will recognise the symptoms easily, a desire to please, an imperative to ensure that no one is unhappy, a smoother of any bother or commotion. I was not a martyr, you understand, I enjoyed doing things for people, it gave me a feeling of satisfaction, of a job well done, well that is what I told myself. My mother was a martyr, everything catalogued, receipted, what she had done for who, the inconvenience caused, how she was never thanked, taken for granted etc. At least I knew I was doing what I was doing because it made me feel good to be of service, plain and simple, I wanted to be wanted and therefore did not begrudge people taking advantage of me, or only a little bit anyway. And it was the only way I was going to get my big English breakfast. And so, food bought, I got on with cooking Chris an amazing never to be forgotten breakfast fit for a king, washed down with lashings of proper hot tea.

Full of breakfast, we wandered up to the pub, where else would we go on a Sunday? Only this time it was a pub called the Hayworth Arms. We arrived promptly at the opening time of midday, it seemed this was traditional. The pub was only open for 2 hours on a Sunday lunchtime, so quite a bit of drinking had to be squeezed into an inconveniently short window.

We arrived outside the Hayworth Arms, a rather grand mock Tudor pub that still stands even now on the corner of the Cottingham and Beverley Roads. Inside were two bars, the lounge with green flock wallpaper and sticky red patterned carpet and the bar with lino and green tiles. There was lots of very dark wood panelling and green velvet upholstery in the lounge, wooden benches, and anaglypta wallpaper in the bar, a fairly standard 80s pub. The velvet seating in the lounge sported the ubiquitous cigarette burns and the holes spewed stuffing. The bar had a darts board and a pool table. Little did I know at that point how well I was going to become acquainted with the Hayworth Arms.

Waiting outside and appearing somewhat jumpy were Dick, Paul and Gary. Sean it seemed had the most normal life of all of them and had gone off to his Mum's for Sunday lunch with the rest of his extended family. Chris was again greeted as a long-lost brother in arms, and I was welcomed with a chorus of 'still got that posh bird in tow then'.

Two hours later, we emerged blinking into the sunlight. Over the next few months, I could not begin to tell you what we talked about for those long lunchtimes and evenings in the pub or huddled on various sofas and chairs in someone's flat or house in between opening hours.

Conversations were wide ranging, about the news, history (Dick's personal mastermind subject), relationships, funny tales of daring do from their younger lives. Either way, there was always something to talk about and plenty to laugh about usually, not counting Gary's situation. Gary was having a particularly bad time of it having not seen his little boy for over 5 weeks. He had been due a supervised visit with a care worker, but on turning up at his ex-wife's house she had been out. He ranted and clenched his fists; she had found the perfect weapon to hurt him with and seemed to wield it with practised ease against him. I suspect that at this stage what might have been best for the little boy had een forgotten by both of them in the battle. Tracey ometimes turned up to the Sunday pub sessions with Dick, depending on whether she had to work or train or s is still the case with nurses, do both at the same time. he hung on Dick's arm and contributed little to the onversation, much of it must have seemed quite alien o her young mind and outlook.

On that first visit to Hull, at about five o'clock after spending the Sunday afternoon in Paul's house, I convinced Chris that there were more interesting things to do and we left. He admitted to me that this was how he spent all of his weekends apart from the ones spent driving to Wales and back and it suited him.

'But it's not real life, Chris. It's just an extension of college isn't it, except with work instead of studying. How do you get up for work every morning if you are drinking every night?"

"Not a problem so far, I have a hangover, but no one seems to notice. I keep my head down until lunchtime, and I usually feel OK in the afternoons."

"You'll be dead before you are thirty the way you are going."

"I'll have had fun though, won't I?" was his wry reply.

The following morning saw me getting onto a National Express Coach at Hull Station for the return journey to Oxford. It had taken us about 3 hours to drive up in Chris's rust heap, the coach was going to take seven glorious fun filled hours to get back to Oxford, followed by another 40 minutes on a local bus after that to get back to my parents. It was an awful, mind-numbing experience. There were no iPads or mobile phones to distract and entertain, I had a dog-eared women's magazine picked up at Smith's at the bus station, and a book that I had hastily grabbed from Chris's flat that turned out not to be my kind of book at all, being some sort of spy thriller thing about a chap called Smiley. Despite the horror of the return journey, over the following six weeks I repeated this journey three times in both directions.

Why? My parents could not understand it and were keen for me to get a job of some sort and move out. I must admit I was finding it hard to understand too. Was I still in love with Chris? The long bus journeys gave me plenty of time to think and work out a reasonably sensible answer to that one, except I never did. I suspected that I might still have been, or I might just have been clutching at the familiar, afraid to set off into the unknown on my own. And I was enjoying belonging to a group of friends, a bit like an extended family.

As I got to know them all a bit better, I became more charitable in my opinions of them and found I enjoyed their company more too. They were all intelligent, witty, mostly self-deprecating, and fun. I like to think I fitted right in, and they seemed to like me, but as usual I was acting on instinct, just doing what ever felt right at the time.

Being offered as the alternative, my parent's market

town, the town of my school days, was boring with all my old school friends thrown to the four winds, it was pretty busy with the Barbour country set and visiting tourists marvelling at the yellow stone buildings, the tea shops and antique shops which proliferated on the high street, all steeped in history.

Going to Hull stopped my father trying to get me to apply to the RAF or the police force, a uniform and three hot meals a day appearing to be being his ambition for me in respect of gainful employment. Although marrying an RAF officer like himself seemed to be a prize one beyond that and joining the RAF the one sure way of achieving this pinnacle of marriage success. I did keep pointing out that I was still married, and that getting married again was not a current ambition. The only RAF officer he managed to get me to go on a blind date with was very nice, but later it came to light that he was gay and sometime after our one and only disastrous date, he was caught in flagrante in his room with a non-commissioned officer, so that didn't go well, particularly as due to the rules at the time he got thrown out of the service.

I was tempted by the police force route, I imagined myself as a mounted policewoman, a joke my father was not impressed by! I simply couldn't say mounted policewoman without dissolving into sniggers. However, the police recruitment office informed me that being able to ride a horse was not a benefit as they would have to retrain me anyway and a prerequisite prior to being mounted (snigger) was two years on the beat. So, my dream of riding football crowds down on a large Irish hunter died as fast as it had been born.

Going to Hull got me out from under my parents' feet and after two years of living in the States; Hull was fun, the rather strange group of people I had met were fun and I hadn't yet worked out what a prat I was making of myself.

CHAPTER FOUR
Move and Be Damned

The Prat Quota rose to an all-time high on my fourth visit. This visit was going to be for a whole week. Chris and I kept agreeing that I wasn't moving in with him, but I could see that day coming when I would arrive and not go back. However, when I arrived on that particular Wednesday everything was fine until the Thursday when a phone call from Morgan put everything out of kilter.

"That was Morgan."

"No really," I remarked sarcastically, I felt confident she would soon be history.

"She has decided that her Dad is on the mend and she can risk a visit up here," he said apologetically.

"You didn't make any attempt to put her off, I notice, it's going to be a bit cosy in the flat with the three of us isn't it?"

"You'll have to go home; I haven't seen her for three months what with her Dad being ill and you being here," he said matter-of-factly.

"Oh, so it is my fault now," I threw at him, "Sorry to get in the way of the romance of the century, but you invited me here. You must have known that this would happen, I expected you to go to her if anything. This is my home now!" I threw at him angrily.

"Come on, Jules, don't be like that, you can come back next week."

I can hear all you women's libbers telling me where I should have told him to stick his next week, his flat, his company and most of all his penis! OK, so pride was not something I seemed to have enough off, and as such I swallowed what little I had and rather than go home I went to camp out in Sean's flat for the weekend, which as he had a new girlfriend was extremely good of him, even if it was a bit awkward!

It transpired that the pub crowd had never met Morgan and that when she had come up to Hull a couple of times, Chris had vanished for the weekend. So, I mused rather anxiously, was the fact that he introduced me to his friends good? Or was it bad that he didn't feel the need to spend 'quality' time with me like he did with Morgan?

I spent the weekend as usual down the pub at every opportunity seething with jealousy and confusion and flirting like crazy with all of Chris's odd friends. As Tracey was away, Dick was an obvious choice for the majority of this and we got on like a house on fire. He started calling me his 'Reserve Girlfriend'. I was stupidly flattered. OK, I thought to myself at a particularly low moment, so I did still love Chris, and I wanted him to be as enthralled with me as he so obviously still was with Morgan and he wasn't and it was at this point that I should have done all the aforementioned sticking (flat, company, penis) and gone back home to not so leafy Oxfordshire never to return.

Instead, I waited humbly for Morgan to return to the Welsh valleys on Sunday afternoon. I did have some sympathy for her at this point as it seems that her National Express Coach journey was 10 hours door to door. I hoped it might stop her returning too quickly. I returned to Chris's flat on the Sunday night as if I had never been away. Although, all power to me, I refused to have sex with him until the sheets had been changed and he had had a bath. Woman's libbers eat your heart out.

As I trailed back to Oxford on the bus the following Wednesday, I realised that things could not go on as they had been, my relationship with National Express Coaches was getting far too permanent. I was exhausted; I couldn't find a job always being on the move. Autumn was well and truly here, and winter was on its way and I couldn't imagine the journey in the dark and the cold thrown in for good measure. So as October arrived, without a great deal of thought (sounds familiar by now doesn't it?), I made the momentous decision to go an live in Kingston-upon-Hull. Whether Chris wanted m to or not, I imagined that I had friends there, a life c sorts beckoned. All I needed was a job, a flat and som transport. Easy! Most of the money I had brought from the States had gone and I had started to sign on fo benefits. I figured I could stay with Chris until I found a job. Chris was amenable, he had got used to having a tidy flat, his washing done, tea on the table and regular sex. I was a frustrated wife-to-be and settled into playing housy-housy for someone who already had a girlfriend and seemed to have no intention of dropping her.

Traipsing around the pubs surrounding Pearson Park one wet and windy October morning yielded a job three nights a week working behind the bar of a small pub called The Queens in a side street off Pearson Park. It was all cash in hand and had the added bonus of stopping me spending my limited funds on drinking in the Swiss Cottage and the Hayworth Arms every night. There was also some dole money coming in, OK so I was a benefit cheat, although I never really thought about it being a bad thing at the time, as it wasn't money you could actually live on, I was just trying to make ends meet and I was able to get by and so I blundered on until Christmas. As well as the pub job, just before Christmas I had applied for a part time teaching post in Hull that Paul had told me was being advertised at the school he worked at. I had taken an extra year after my degree to do a Post Graduate Certificate of Education (PGCE) at the same University, this rather brief introduction to teaching qualified me as a probationary teacher. The PGCE allowed me to impart geographical knowledge to children from 11 to 16 years which was good news for the teaching job in Hull, but maybe not good news for the poor kids if by some strange chance I got the job. I had done the PGCE not because I desperately wanted to be a teacher, but so that I could stay with my University Boyfriend who still had another year of his degree to do, really clear thinking as usual. My parents had supported what they thought was a proper career choice, and to cap it all, I got an additional year's grant (which we didn't have to pay back in those days). I don't think my University Boyfriend would thank me for plastering his name all over this so I will continue to refer to him as University Boyfriend. He had been the boy I met and spent all the rest of my university time with after the first two terms when Chris and I had gone to worms. University Boyfriend healed my heart and our relationship turned into a committed and passionate one in a very short period of time.

This extra year at university had been followed in the summer by a trip to the USA via BUNAC to be a camp counsellor in Maine (think *Friday the 13th*, cabins among the pine trees, a beautiful lake, complete silence at night). Pine Lake Camp for girls is where I had met my first husband, the nice American called Tom. This was where I tried to teach swimming and horse riding to American girls aged 8-16, predominately from rich families. Meeting Tom at the girl's camp that his family owned was the death knell for my relationship with University Boyfriend, not quite out of sight, out of mind, but I was angry and upset with him for not going travelling with me which fuelled my interest in Tom.

Tom was the only single man in a camp of 20 female counsellors and 150 girls. I didn't get on that well with women of any age, I was scared witless by them, but boys I could communicate with. Tom was a lovely man, handsome in a dark skinny way, the camp tennis coach, everyone loved him, particularly all of the 150 girls over 13, and so with my low self-esteem seeking constant reassurance, I envisaged a rather lovely holiday romance, fluffy and not really important, and that worked out well! Even now when I think of University Boyfriend and how it all ended, it fills me with regret and even after all this time I have a great fondness for him still and the great university time we had together. University Boyfriend rang my parent's house a few days before my wedding to Tom to say he had heard I was getting married, but that he still loved me and would I change my mind.

Things like that only happen in films don't they, except in this case it was my life. I cried a lot, having had the epiphany that I also still loved University Boyfriend. Tom was confused by the tears, I was confused by them, my mother was clear – the wedding was to go ahead, people I didn't know, close friends of my parents were already travelling including Tom's mother and best man from the US, money had been spent. That was it, no arguments, it went ahead, and for the most part was a happy day.

Once I make a decision, I commit to it wholeheartedly and so I put the call from University Boyfriend behind me, and Tom and happy ever after fairly and squarely in my sights, not that it helped in the end, but I was sincere. I realised now that I should have grabbed the chance to get back to University Boyfriend, despite the hurt and recriminations that might have followed, but I was not very strong in the face of my mother and Tom. Still, University Boyfriend and Tom are both different sad stories that brought me to this place and I have been wallowing in the regrets of the past (of which there are many) and digressing from the story in hand.

I enjoyed the Christmas of 1982; I had missed my family as the one before had been spent in the US. Chris drove us both home from Hull, I spent it with my parents and three brothers, all of us home from various places. Chris spent Christmas with his family and then New Year in Wales with Morgan. We drove back north on the third of January, to take up where we had left off on December 23rd.

I returned to the news that I had got the teaching job, which might have been something to do with Paul putting in a good word for me, or they were desperate as I can't think of any other reason they would have taken on a trainee teacher with zero experience, I started immediately after Christmas.

It was in a school across the river in East Hull, a large mixed ability comprehensive housed in the standard glass encased sixties blocks probably riddled with asbestos and with leaky roofs. It was arranged in a square campus with glass covered tunnels between the building. The school was drab and defeated, the staff were drab and defeated, the children mostly uninterested and hostile, but as it was a temporary position, when I was interviewed and offered it, I took it. I was to cover for a female teacher who had run off with one of her 15-year-old pupils. The general feeling was that the boy had scored and little or no harm would come of it, or to him. The reverse situation would have course have elicited a completely different reaction from the world even then, and this created much heated debate in our Friday lunchtime sessions in the pub when we had made it exhausted almost to the end of the teaching week.

Drinking at lunchtime with work colleagues has since gone out of fashion, going back to school to finish an afternoon teaching after a couple of pints is now frowned upon. Shame. Different times.

Having the teaching job and the pub job gave me a reasonable and a regular salary allowing me to stop claiming dole and to start to look for a flat of my own, as I decided I could not face the ignominy of sofa

ırfing when the feted Morgan came to see Chris. Chris
id nothing to dissuade me, or he didn't try very hard
nyway, and I reasoned that with Morgan on the scene
: at least gave me back my dignity.

found a second floor, one bedroomed flat on one of
he avenues off Pearson Park, it was small but nice, fully
urnished with the required living room, bedroom,
oathroom and kitchen, there was a big communal
garden out the back too. I was going to struggle to
afford it, but I was determined to free myself from the
very destructive situation with Chris, which was going
nowhere. I needed to call his bluff. He double bluffed
my bluff and helped me move my stuff in his car in the
first week of February when I moved in. We christened
my new flat with a bonk.

We lay in bed afterwards gazing at the ceiling,

"You didn't have to get this flat you know," Chris
remarked idly, "I thought it was going pretty well with
you at my place?"

"Yeah, until the next time Morgan decided to visit."

"Well, you know, that's a little difficult, her dad is
dying, the last thing she needs is to be dumped by me."

"So, are you are going to dump her then? How long
do you wait after the funeral to dump her? I just think
that you want to keep the both of us, me dangling on a
string, her blissfully ignorant, and so I can't really think
of you as my boyfriend. This is my first time living on
my own, I intend to enjoy it, be independent, and that
means from you too." What a speech. My tone was firm,

adamant even, the new me emerging?

"No more bonking then?" was his response, prioritie
quite clear. I loved how simply he saw life, he never le
his massive intellect get in the way of his cock.

"Well, I may not go that far," I backtracked, "I
depends if anyone else comes along."

I didn't believe at the time that anyone else woulc
come along, I just wanted to let him have a taste of his
own medicine. I really believed that I just had to bide
my time and Morgan would be gone and all would be
well.

CHAPTER FIVE

Life On My Own, Apart From a Puppy

I settled into my new flat, it was the first time I had ever truly lived on my own and I was mostly enjoying it, but it could be lonely without anyone there when I was feeling a little low. The teaching was hell, worse than hell, I had absolutely no control over the children, and it got to the point where I would cry quietly to myself each morning as I got ready to cycle to the school. I was only going three days a week, but even that was getting hard to do. Paul had very kindly given me his old racing bike, it was a little too tall for me and the racing position not quite what I needed, but beggars can't be choosers.

In the days before cycle lanes and bike helmets, I was taking my life into my hands every morning and evening in the dark and the wet. Did I say it rained a lot in Hull? It rained a lot in Hull! The cycling was also giving me thighs of thunder, they grew so quickly with the exercise that I ended up with stretch marks on them as my skin failed to keep up, how crap is that?

Now actually in a real school, I realised how little my one year of training, which included 4 weeks in an actual school, had prepared me for a class of 40 teenagers. I spent most of the day shouting 'quiet, quiet!,' ' Sit Down!' and 'Listen to me!' to no avail. Hearing the ruckus, a proper teacher would knock and wander in and there would be silence in about 4 seconds. Humiliating didn't really do it justice. To give me some due, there were children in my class who could do the set work in 10 minutes and others who couldn't read. The girls could be lovely, but the 15-year-old boys tried to hit on me, probably because they had seen it work once with my predecessor, or maybe just because they were 15 year old boys and I was young and reasonably attractive.

Which government said mixed ability classes were a good idea? In my humble and inexperienced opinion, this could only work with unlimited resources and small class sizes, oh and good teachers, which counted me out. But at the same time as this, I had swapped evening jobs from The Queens to the Hayworth Arms. As this was the pub that Chris and his cronies inhabited most evenings, I got to see what was going on and keep up with the gossip as I strolled around collecting glasses, emptying overflowing ashtrays and wiping a grimy cloth over the table while everyone held glasses and bear mats up out of the way.

Onto the next mistake, there must be another one, this is my life, remember? I took it to the next level and decided that I had to have a dog because I was lonely. We'd had two dogs as children, Pongo (named after the famous Dalmatian, of course) who had to be put down as he caught the dog equivalent of venereal disease, and then a mongrel called Timmy who had been run down when I was 13 and he was less than a year old. I knew nothing of caring for a dog, but any self-respecting adult who was out 3 days and 3 evenings and Saturday lunchtimes needed a dog, didn't they?

This was also the days before such luxuries as dog walkers, not that I could have afforded one. I lied to the dog rescue folk about only working a few hours in the evening, they didn't check (they have sharpened up their act now, thank goodness), so he was mine. He was a 12-week-old black Labrador-cross puppy with a small white triangle on his chest and as the Star Wars phenomenon had just hit the big screen, I decided to call him Vadar (after Darth, do you see what a genius I was?) I was certain that whatever Chris felt, Vadar loved me totally and completely and made my life complete.

The fact that I lived in a small flat on the second floor was of course neither here nor there. I took him out in the early morning for a little walk and toilet break and came home at about 4pm from school and did the same, of course in between he had crapped and piddled everywhere and had probably been desperately unhappy and lonely too, so who could blame the little fella? I mopped it up and sighed, and waited for him to be house-trained. I settled into a routine as the first term at school came to an end and I breathed a sigh of relief to have two weeks off for Easter, this helped me to get on top of the house-training and to try hard to not think about going back to school for another term.

Meanwhile in the real world, not inhabited by man-eating tigers and piddling puppies, Sean's old girlfriend Clare also came back from the States where she had been doing something much more glamorous and exciting than me for the previous year. It seems that she had also gone out with Dick for a while when his wife left him. Clare was a tall, beautiful, artistic brunette and right from the first meeting seemed very taken with Chris. Apart from Gary, the rest of the men in the group were all spoken for, so despite being spoken for twice if you counted me, Chris was the next obvious conquest for her. He didn't put up much of a fight, I think her artistic side called to him as he painted and drew quite brilliantly. Or it might have been the very impressive breasts, much rarer in the 80s than now.

And remembering my words about us not really going out (was that me who said that?), he began to respond to her attentions, and they started to hang out together quite a lot, with me stuck the other side of the bar most of the time. I could only watch miserably as he brought in large carrots and carved them into amazingly lifelike cocks (not male chickens!), veins and everything, impress her. I wondered what the hell I was going to do about it. How had I got into this situation where I had started a new life in a completely new town in the north all because in my heart I wanted to be with my old boyfriend from school, but was now too proud to try to change what was happening in front of me? Clare was a force to be reckoned with, and I didn't have a reckoning bone in my body.

Life settled into a rhythm in the first half of 1983. I still cried every morning I had to go to school because trying to be a teacher was so dreadfully hard. Despite the long holidays I had dreamed of, I now know that it is a vocation, so well done all you teachers out there, you really deserve those holidays.

Vadar got bigger and more badly behaved, but I still loved him. Even with Vader in it, my flat seemed to get lonelier, and the group of people I hung around with got stranger, and Chris spent most of his free time with Clare.

The teaching was going really badly, and I was trying to hang in there for the second term. On realising it was not my future, I did something my father was very pleased about, which was apply to the graduate entry scheme for the Civil Service. It was a bit like a university application, I got to pick three government departments and I would join one as an Executive Officer, or EO as they were known, the first management grade in the civil service at the time.

How much thought do you think I gave these choices that could govern the rest of my life? Very little, to be honest. I picked Customs and Excise as my first choice as I really fancied the idea of busting drugs barons at the port, and assumed I would get my first choice which for someone with my luck is pretty strange. I randomly picked the Department of Agriculture and The Department of Science and Education as my other choices. If I got the job, it could be anywhere in the country, depending on when posts came free. It would mean leaving Hull, but I was thinking to hell with Chris, to hell with Hull. Also, I had been told that the selection process could take up to a year as I had to take an exam and attend an interview panel all of which only happened at certain times of the year. I posted my application and thought no more of it, well why would I?

Around this time, maybe to get back at Chris, I can't be certain of my motives now, but I am sure that loneliness also came into it; I also took up romantically with someone else. A bloke who regularly came into the Hayworth Arms, called Rob. As he was a trade union official down at a local steelworks and because he also carried around a copy of the 'Socialist Worker', he was known affectionately as 'Red Rob' to my friends. He had been coming into the Hayworth Arms and staying at the bar instead of sitting with his mates, talking to me in-between me serving rounds, but as I had to add up the rounds in my head and it was a very busy city pub, he didn't get to say much. He was tall, blond, blue-eyed and handsome. We flirted a lot, and he always bought me a drink at the end of the night, so when he asked me out, I said yes. I can't remember where we went on our first date, but I suspect it was my flat as he still lived at home with his parents. He was a nice bloke and OK in the bonking department, and very nice to me. This should have been warning enough that it would not last, but he distracted me from Chris and Clare and their blossoming relationship, one I know was upsetting the two exes: Sean and Dick, as much as me. Although Sean's current girlfriend seemed very pleased about it – some people can be so cruel.

About a month into going out, Rob invited me to attend a Rugby League match with him, and I was told by his friends that he had never done this before. I started to worry that he was much more serious about our relationship than I was. He was very fond of Vadar, and made me proper full English northern breakfasts on a Sunday, including cooking mushrooms in tea!

Things got decided at the match. It was freezing, the rules were undecipherable, and the pies disgusting. There were two Rugby league teams in Hull, one each side of the river, A red one and a blue one is the best I could tell you. He supported the blue one. He wrapped his blue and white scarf around my neck and gave me a kiss on the terraces in front of all his mates.

Time to run for the hills, me thinks.

I am not an unkind person, I dumped him gently,

telling him we were from two different worlds (it was clichés week after all), that it had been fun but time to go our different ways, dropping in that I had voted for Maggie at the last election (well if we are being honest, my Dad had wielded my proxy vote on my behalf as I was in the US and as such I was sure it would have been true blue Tory). I think that was the clincher, he left thinking he had had a very close Tory shave and it was for the best for certain.

And then it was just me and Vadar again, smiling through gritted teeth while my best friend and erstwhile lover got it on with someone else with much bigger breasts than me.

CHAPTER SIX

Dick Anyone?

As we got into the late spring of 1983, Chris started to look for a house to buy in Hull.

"I have got some houses to go and look at," he said casually to me in the pub one Sunday lunchtime waving some brochures at me. "I could do with a woman's point of view, I am not very good at that sort of thing."

I was confused by his motive, given that I had no more idea about buying a house than he did and was sure our criteria would be completely different. Also, he was still seeing Morgan, and Clare as well now, and not me at all, not even casually. I thought (wildly and stupidly, see there I go again) that as Morgan's dad had died recently that he might ask me to live with him and that was why he wanted me to house hunt with him. I thought that if he did then I would.

"Why don't you ask Clare?" I said casually back, she wasn't around so I was on safe ground,

"Don't want her getting the wrong idea do I?" he explained. But it was OK if I did? Sigh!

"Are you going to stop seeing Morgan," I challenged.

"No, not at the moment, it is still too soon after her dad dying, she is in pieces still," he countered.

"Count me out of the house hunting," I said. How long could this all go on? I needed a plan of my own. Man-eating tiger warning! It was at about this time that Dick the teacher was dumped by his girlfriend Tracey, given the age and intelligence gap, no one was surprised. And therefore, he called in his reserve, who was me, of course. It was early, about 6pm, just after opening and there were just the two of us so far.

"The reserve thing," he started.

"Yes, it's a good joke right?"

"Not a joke to me, I really like you, we could go out?"

"Oh," I was a bit lost for words. "Yes, we could see how it goes," I replied non-committally.

He slid his arm along the back of the banquette and leant forward and very gently kissed me on the lips.

"Oh!" I said again, something was fluttering! He was handsome, sincere, kind, funny and oh so charming. Before I knew what had happened, I had gone along with it, and snuggled into the offered arm. If you are wondering what he saw in me, well I was personable and intelligent, and considered attractive. I was tall, 5 foot 9 inches, with an athletic build (nothing to do ith exercise) slim but without the impressive breasts, shoulder length dark blond hair, green eyes, quite impressive cheek bones and a small nose, a pretty rather than beautiful face.

In terms of attractiveness quotient – we matched, which is always helpful in relationships, I think. We never had a proper date, he never took me anywhere other than the Swiss Cottage and the Hayworth Arms, but before I knew it, I was Dick's official girlfriend, no longer his reserve and in the space of a month I had OK sex with him and stayed over at his flat quite a few nights. On the back of the early success of it all, after about 6 weeks, as the end of the summer term approached, me and Vader were living full time with him in his flat. This allowed me to give up my flat which since I was giving up my teaching job at the end of the term, I could not afford, so to me it made sense.

All eggs were very firmly in one basket, make or break, go for broke. When I committed to something, I really committted, I think I said that before, didn't I? Great news for Vader, as not only was I home during the day but he had a garden too. And to be honest, I didn't actually give up the teaching job voluntarily. I had an assessment and was not awarded my full teaching certificate on the back of the performance. I was told that I would need to do at least six more months of probation to get my teaching certificate. The writing was on the wall, teaching was not for me.

Ending up at Dick's flat seemed to be a good solution

to all those problems, that or go home to my parents an[d] start again (Oh, if only I had). With Clare and Morga[n] still so firmly in the picture, I saw very little of Chri[s] but I wasn't ready to not be in the same town as him. [I] didn't think of the thing with Dick as serious, not love just expedient and he was good company – to start with anyway.

To set the scene of my life for the months that followed; Dick lived in a one bedroom ground floor flat on Beresford Road, literally a two minute walk from the Hayworth Arms. They were old Victorian terraced two-story houses of the less grand variety, with small front and back gardens, just one room wide. Many had been converted into flats and studios. Dick's flat was at the back on the ground floor and was the largest in the house.

When Dick had been married previously, he had got as far as buying a nice new box on a modern estate for himself and his family. I think he'd had good prospects as his wife had been a teacher too. A nice life by most people's standards, but he had blown it and at the age of 35, he was very much on his uppers, living the life of someone much younger and poorer than he actually was. He still had a good salary as a deputy head of department at his school, but he spent it furiously on drink, his pigeons (yes he had pigeons, more about them later) and going out, so never seemed to have any spare cash.

I assumed, and no one dissuaded me of the facts, that his wife had left him and gone back to Lancaster because of his drinking and hanging around with his mates all the time. The two of them had been together since teacher training college in Hull, so it must have been hard for him to now be living the single life again and not seeing his little girl. He seemed to think she was better off without him, or maybe Lancaster was just too far away. He didn't drive and turned out not to be great at travelling away from Hull, so Lancaster might as well have been on the moon. He didn't have a passport and had never been on aeroplane at the time I met him.

Dick's ground floor flat had a large living room and a large kitchen with a bathroom off it as well as a roomy bedroom. It was furnished with second hand tatty furniture that had come with the flat and a few meagre belongings. His ex-wife obviously had the contents of their family home. There was a sagging three-seater sofa and an old leather chair in the living room with a large veneer covered coffee table in front.

He had posters rather than pictures on the wall, mostly from *Lord of the Rings* and *Dune* and other science fantasy books, but an old photo I found revealed a Snoopy poster too. Being on the ground floor it also had the garden. Although the word 'garden' is a bit grand as it was filled with heaps of rubbish and rubble everywhere and also contained a pigeon loft where Dick kept his racing pigeons.

It was early June when I moved in, but later the

flat proved to be freezing, as it only had one gas fire in the living room, and a very dodgy gas water and wall heater in the bathroom and a gas water heater in the kitchen. No carbon dioxide detectors in the 80s, so I was probably risking life and limb every time I turned it on to have a bath. It was quite a tidy flat, everything in its place and a place for everything, lots and lots of bookcases filled with books, but under the neatness it was also filthy. Not again, I thought as on my first day there, once I finished school and had some time on my hands, I rolled up my sleeves and began to clean.

I cleaned and scrubbed and tidied and turned his little shithole flat into a home. I hoovered carpets that had never been hoovered, with a hoover that had never been emptied, my first challenge being to empty the existing bag so it could be reused as there were no new ones. I washed the kitchen floor that I am fairly certain had never been washed in the two years that Dick had lived there. The bathroom walls were coated in black mould, this was all scrubbed off too. Without a job, I had plenty of time to get everything sanitary. Soon all was pristine, and Dick acted as if it had always been that way.

And so there I was playing house again. I detect a theme. A search for stability and a home of my own. I was an RAF brat (term of affection) and as such we had moved house every 3 years all through my childhood, finally settling in Oxfordshire, but it was not until about 1972 and I was 14 that my parents had owned their first house. Don't get me wrong, I had lived in Cyprus and

Singapore and had quite a happy, interesting childhood, but due to all the moving I had no idea how to make friends and also had no sense of where I belonged as we moved around so much. I wanted so much to feel that I was home, that I belonged, that I was safe. I thought that I might find that with Dick, but we both seemed to be people looking for connection and relationship in the wrong place.

Being an animal lover (I had a dog after all, even if he was delinquent) I started to help Dick look after the pigeons. I felt a bit sorry for them as they were neglected by him. He had about 12 of them and they were breeding at the time I arrived. As time went on and I learnt more about racing pigeons and Dick spent more time in the pub without me, I became their sole carer. At the time I started in the summer of 1983, there were ugly little featherless chicks everywhere.

Once a day in the evening Dick would let the adult birds out and off they would go soaring into the sky as a flock, belting around the house, before returning 30 minutes later to their chicks or eggs, worn out. They returned because their mate, chicks or eggs were in the loft. They would try to do this from over 300 miles away if necessary.

To those uninitiated into the world of racing pigeons, i.e. pretty much everyone, this will require more explanation. If Dick was ever to race his pigeons, it was to be on the 'Widower system'. Cock and hen birds were mated up and allowed to lay eggs. Equality rules in the pigeon marriage and the cock bird shares egg sitting in shifts of 12 hours each with the hen. So, if he or she are taken a long way away for a race, they will break heaven and earth to return to the loft and not let their partner down. We could learn a lot from racing pigeons. And luckily, they mostly seem to have an unerring sense of direction in terms of returning home from a long way away, it wouldn't be much of a sport without that ability, to be honest.

I used to imagine the pigeon conversations when the cock bird finally returned victorious or otherwise.

"Where the hell have you been, do you know it is your turn to sit on these bloody eggs? I have been here without a break now for 18 hours. I should have listened to my mother, she warned me about cocks like you."

Big sigh from cock, "Sorry dear, I got back as fast as I could."

Dick's pigeons never raced once in all of the time that I knew him. Why? Well the biggest flaw in Dick being a pigeon racer was that races were on Saturdays and Sundays, and when he should have been waiting at the loft for the returning birds to be clocked back in using a special machine using their leg ring, he was down the pub. They ended up being pets, and like most pets, what they did most was eating and crapping, and when it came to crap, I was an expert, as you must well know by now.

With the teaching job now history, I continued to work behind the bar at the Hayworth Arms, but also managed to get another part time job to keep the wolf from the door while waiting for the Customs and Excise job to drop into my lap as I felt sure it would. I had seen the new job advertised at the job centre, it was at the Library of the local YTS College. The Youth Training Scheme was for 16-year-old school leavers, cheap labour and a bit of training in a vocational job, a sort of apprentice scheme except the government paid the employers to take on the youngsters.

I applied to work at the YTS library and surprisingly was offered the job. I worked four afternoons a week which also worked with Vader as once Dick went back to work in September, he was home from school at about 4.30 in the afternoon. The library was mostly deserted, and I would sort out books, arrange shelves, and type up new index cards (no computers in those days). I made displays on various life skills such as opening a bank account, budgeting, job interviews, how to rent a flat. I don't think the students paid much attention to them, but they appealed to my limited creativity. As there was a catering section to the college, cheap and rather nice food was cooked and served by the students at lunchtime before I started work, so I ate rather well too.

Dick did not ask for rent, I am guessing the cleaning, cooking and sex were considered enough so I had enough money to enjoy myself with no responsibilities and started to think about saving up for a car. Life was grand! I had been in Hull for 9 months by then, and was living with Dick for 3 months when it began to occur to me that all this part time working and hand to mouth existence was not as grand as I made out, and not particularly fulfilling either. Waiting for the Civil Service job was becoming a subject of anxiety, would it ever happen?. The librarian job would go nowhere as I didn't have the right qualifications to be a proper librarian and I was wondering what my options were now that teaching was off the table.

In case you're wondering, my 3rd class honours degree was in Geology and of no use to me at all, unless I wanted to head up to Aberdeen to work on the oil rigs and at the time, they didn't allow women on them. Just as I was despairing of my chances of getting a full-time proper job, my application to be a civil servant started to have some legs.

In November, I was called over to Leeds to take an exam with about 400 other people in a large hall, mostly literacy and numeracy, and I remember I had to write an essay on something. I must have passed it because I was called back a few weeks later to take a computer literacy test. No one had asked me if I wanted to work in IT. It wasn't called IT then, it was called Computing, but having taken the exam I was declared to be perfect Computing material. Who'd have guessed it? I was completely number illiterate when it came to mathematics, having failed my O' Level three times, (something now known quite grandly as Dyscalculia), but I learnt that being in IT was more about logic than sums, so I tried not to worry about my lack of arithmetic abilities.

Having passed the exam and the IT test, next was an interview by a panel, but I was warned this could take several months to come through. So I decided to carry on at the library and behind the bar of the Hayworth Arms while I waited and life went on.

The pub work was OK, I worked there three nights a week and one lunchtime in the Hayworth, and then sat in the Hayworth on several other nights and spent what I had earned. Dick was having a love affair with his new video recorder that had cost him £400, a huge sum of money at that time.

The pair of us would sit down each afternoon with the Radio Times magazine to decide what to record onto our video tapes to watch when we returned from the pub. We had vastly different tastes. I was a *Dallas*, *Cheers* and sitcom comedy fan, Dick preferred documentaries and news programmes along with cricket, snooker and football. We would ring what we wanted to watch in red pen, and he would set up the recordings which was very complicated and only he could do. When we were not watching recorded TV on endless video tapes, we went to the pub. We entertained sometimes; the pub crew would come around on a Saturday afternoon with a box from the Offy. Sean would bring his new girlfriend, quite a crowd. I would even cook for them all; a one-pot mince stew was favourite, or egg and chips.

We talked rubbish for hours, as if we were the most interesting people in the world, after which we would head to the pub again, me to work sometimes, them to drink. We even went out to parties occasionally and to clubs sometimes. I loved to dance. Sean was an amazing dancer, we all hit the dance floor together, fun was being had in spades. The only fly in the ointment was that Chris was there with Clare sometimes. It was uncomfortable for me, there were too many 'exes' in the room for both of them, but we muddled along being nice to each other.

This was a normal state of affairs, but I had heard that she was giving him grief over Morgan. Touche! But that was their business. I thought I was happy, content even, and Chris was most definitely in the past now.

CHAPTER SEVEN

In Which the Sh*t Hits the Fan

Things changed early the following year as we heralded in the famous 1984 without the clocks striking 13. Christmas at my mum and dad's had come and gone, work was OK, Dick and I had settled into a domestic routine and I felt happy and settled. Even though the flat was freezing in the winter and we spent a long time huddled in front of the electric fire, I was having a pretty good run of normality, and everything was too good to be true.

That all changed one Sunday at about 6pm. Traditionally, we went to the pub on Sunday evenings, to the back bar of the Hayworth to play darts. On this particular Sunday night, there was something on the TV I wanted to watch, so I wanted to stay home. I didn't want to go out into the cold and the wet, so I tried to persuade Dick to stay home with me. I realise now that this was not going to happen ever. Dick made a point of never drinking in the house unless we had company, and as such, if he didn't go out, he didn't get a drink and the drink was calling him. This must have made him quite tense, and I was an angry bee buzzing in the way of his goal. I persisted, nagged, stood close in front of him, delivering words of disagreement into his face and then he hit me hard, just once.

His fist connecting with my chin were accompanied by the words, "We are going to the pub, so just shut up, will you?"

I had never experienced violence in my life. I brought my hand up to my face and began to cry, shocked and shaken. I had known this man for 9 months and that he was capable of this had never ever occurred to me, it seemed impossible.

He didn't say sorry, he just said, "We're leaving in 15 minutes, be ready, OK?"

I mumbled "OK," and headed for the bathroom to stare at my reflection in the mirror. There was no outward sign of damage, although the following day a small bruise would appear on my cheekbone. One of my front teeth felt a little loose and I found this worried me, even more than the fact that the man I now loved and lived with had struck me. I didn't even think about not going to the pub, I was shocked into compliance, deflated and defeated. He was right and I was in the wrong. This was the first time in my life that I had been ruck by another human being. My mum and dad could wield sharp words, undermining confidence, but they never hit us. I feel suspended, unreal and somehow untouched by what had happened. It was so far outside my understanding of the world that I was unable to assimilate it or respond to it. I realise now that I was in hock, but at the time, I thought that it meant I had no feelings, or that what Dick had done was OK, perfectly reasonable, in fact.

"Are we going to the pub or not?" he said from the bathroom door, seemingly unperturbed by what had just happened. Lightbulb moment, I realised at that point that he had probably done this before, his wife and her exit now made more sense. None of his friends had ever said anything, so I thought I might be wrong, but either way it was completely unacceptable and so in my head I started to work out where I would go when I left tomorrow.

My mind was racing with these plans as I followed him numbly out of the door. My jaw ached, but otherwise there was no sign anything had happened and the rest of the evening in the pub went as normal. We played darts, drank and even laughed. I continued to feel dazed and unreal.

Later when we returned to the flat, he said he was sorry, that he had been very tense and still drunk from the lunchtime session and just lashed out. We made love; he was very tender and gentle. I told myself that it was a one off, that I just needed to understand him a bit better. Except of course it wasn't.

Over the next few weeks, he hit me twice more in the face over silly disagreements and once pulled me around the bedroom by my hair. Another time he held me against the wall with his hand around my throat. This was always when he had been drinking, usually late at night. I cannot explain now to anyone who asks why I didn't leave right there and then. We weren't married, we didn't have children. But I stayed put. When he was sober and being nice, he was very nice, kind, funny, and sexy. I thought my life was interesting, in an interesting sort of way. I was afraid of being seen as a failure, particularly by my parents. Running home to them for a second time seemed inconceivable.

Also, there was never any outward sign of his violence towards me and as far as I knew, no one knew about it and so at least in public I didn't have to feel ashamed that I stayed, although I did feel ashamed that I stayed. Most of the time, he seemed to be able to rein it in enough to not do anything that left marks, so it could be put to the back of my mind, not forgiven and forgotten exactly, just processed so I could move on afterwards.

I didn't know then but know now, that violence in a relationship, usually but not exclusively towards a woman, is a constant in our society. Through time, in some people, it is what rises to the surface and it has varying degrees too, up to and including murder. I never felt at that time that Dick would ever hurt me badly but knowing that was not a good reason to stay even though

I did.

In broken relationships it can be a lifetime of belittling, of coercive control, or of being ignored, or of affairs, there are many ways that people can be cruel.

At that time, domestic violence was much more an undercover, behind closed doors thing, a shameful thing, something to hide. It still is now too, but there are more escape channels and external help and more public acknowledgement. Wife battering, girlfriend battering, any kind of battering, bullying, including gas-lighting and other psychological harms; once a protagonist has got away with it once, and made a point with violence or mental cruelty, got their own way using fists or cruel words, it becomes addictive and quickly habitual and may escalate with each successive relationship.

Maybe it is the power over another person's life, maybe it's the feeling of power, maybe it just seems the right way for things to be because often that is how it was for them as a child and so it feels comfortable. Also, there is that release from not feeling that they need to control themselves, that it is OK to behave that way if the victim doesn't call them out.

Certainly for Dick, his violence was driven by all of these things. His drinking lowered his inhibitions and made the line between acceptable and unacceptable very wavy. His dad was a drinker and a bully and had hit his mother hard and often in front of Dick. Over the next couple of months, I learnt a lot about what made Dick flip or not and started to moderate my behaviour to avoid conflict and it worked in that the violence was sporadic, almost half-hearted, as if he was acting out something that he didn't really believe in. I tried very hard to be what he wanted me to be, to make it work. Again, I couldn't begin to tell you why, sorry I can't offer explanations for why I stayed to you or maybe more importantly to myself. I don't think I was happy, just accepting and docile, probably still in shock. Maybe now they would call it PTSD. I know I started to have anxiety attacks that left me gasping and unable to breathe until I managed to calm myself down.

Gradually, probably because I didn't hide it as well as I thought I was, or maybe because Dick had had previous (he had told me the real reason his wife had left him), I realised that the group of friends I was with all knew what was happening. I was embarrassed, I think they were too, I stopped going to the pub with Dick as much as I had, pleading work in the morning or tiredness from working in the pub. I would stay home and colour in big posters with felt pens. I found it relaxing and it took me away from where I was to somewhere where I didn't have to think or feel. I found it quite amusing a few years back to see it becoming a thing called mindfulness with adult colouring books instead of posters.

There were still nice things about those times that I remember balancing out the bad moments. I enjoyed looking after the pigeons, the gentle cooing when I went into the loft, the rustle of the feathers as the birds settled onto perches and nests and the babies, so ugly and so greedy.

I gradually reclaimed that awful mess that was a garden, under the rubble and the rubbish was the bones of a long-ago garden. I borrowed tools from Paul and dug it all out, finding paving and paths and little walls, trimming the hedge and bought plants and brought it back to life. It started a lifelong love of gardening. We all sat outside in a motley assortment of chairs during that summer of 1984 and even had a barbeque once or twice. I remember Sean wielding a pair of tongs in an impossibly small pair of shorts, I have a photo somewhere. Dick had bought a camcorder and he liked to film us as we all hung out.

Occasionally, we all packed into a couple of cars and went off to Beverley or some other not so far flung outpost for a drink or a visit. Or down to the docks and the town for a wander and a drink. We also went out in the evening to house parties and a few times to the local disco for a dance, where Sean would give John Travolta a run for his money and me and Dick could do a pretty good job of disco too. I would also spend quiet times walking Vader up to the fields at the end of Beresford Avenue. They were only playing fields, but having grown up in the country they fed a need in me for space and greenery and air. Vader loved running around and ignoring me as I vainly tried to get him to come back to me.

During the August, I made the long trek by bus and

train back to my university for a 5-year reunion. It was bittersweet, my old University Boyfriend was on my mind a lot, memories of him and our two years together around every corner. Memories of Chris too, memories of good times had, a much easier more carefree time.

One bit of good news at this time, was that Chris was not seeing Clare anymore, which I was jealously pleased about. Although he wasn't house hunting either, he seemed to have settled into a worrying inertia which involved drinking a lot and not being around as much as he had been. I missed him when I remembered, but I had made my decision not to wait for him to see the sense of our relationship, accepting that it was not happily ever after for him and me.

One day in June, he came around the flat when Dick was out at the pub, planned, I guess. A month earlier, Chris had been in a drunken smash in his car, driving into a row of parked cars in the early hours. He had left the scene, only going to the police station in the morning. He had been charged with leaving the scene of an accident, not drunken driving as he should have been, no one had been hurt luckily, but now it had cost him his job and so his flat and his entire life in Hull and he was leaving. He had sat in the pub and told us all he was off to Algeria of all places to teach science at a college there.

At the time I couldn't make sense of what this meant for me, for him and me, reminding myself as always that there was no him and me, that it was me and Dick now.

s he stood there in the living room saying his goodbye, e tried very hard to persuade me to pack and go with im back to Oxfordshire that night.

"What are you doing, Jules?" he exclaimed, "You are orth more than this. Leave now, come with me, I will ake you back to your folks, they will understand," he aid. "It is really hard for me to leave you here with him, lease come away!"

"Algeria, Chris," I choked back through the tears. 'Could you get any further away if you tried?"

"Yes, the States!" he flung back, "I can't stay after what I have done, no job, no car, no flat, a criminal record. I am lucky, my dad has pulled a lot of strings to get me this job in Algeria, think of it as a punishment if that makes you feel better."

It didn't, I stood there crying, thinking about trying to pack in a hurry, what to do with Vader, it all seemed too difficult to do on the spur of the moment. Chris wasn't with Clare, but Morgan was still in the picture, and this hardened my resolve. I was too proud to take his help and his very good advice and I told him I was OK and he shrugged and gave me a massive rib cracking hug and left.

That was the last time I saw Chris for several years, and I remember crying quietly in the bedroom for a very long time after he left. It seemed that the choice was made, I had found my very own leg-chewing tiger and it suited me down to the ground. For one thing, I could blame all of the deficiencies in my life and in myself

on my situation. I could keep myself exactly where
was and never expect any more or have to do anymore
Blissful abdication. Everything that happened from now
on would be Dick's fault, he was now the master of my
destiny, and I was along for the ride.

CHAPTER EIGHT

Escape!

I carried on living with Dick in his flat, and alongside all the nice things I did, homemaking, taking Vader down to the local park, socialising, gardening; I was still enduring low level violence on a weekly basis, or whenever I didn't spot the triggers and modify my behaviour enough to keep a lid on it.

I ran away at one point, and camped out with Gary for a few days, but the only real friend I had was Chris and he had gone. I was just too ashamed to go home to my parents and also, I had Vader to worry about, although that was all about to change. An escalation in Dick's behaviour was that when being aggressive towards me didn't get him the result he wanted, he had started to be violent towards Vader. I know now that this is very common in abusive relationships, that the abuser will start to further harm and manipulate their victim by being cruel towards any children or pets that they have. If he didn't have a good enough excuse to be violent towards me (he was such a fair-minded abuser), then he turned his eyes to Vader. Vadar was always getting in the way, following us about, wanting to be with us, trying to please. He was an easy target, and it had the added bonus of really upsetting me as I tried to protect him from being hit or kicked or being thrown out into the rain. I knew that even if I didn't want to save myself, I was responsible for Vader and so had to save him.

One day after Dick had been particularly brutal to Vader, I grabbed Vader's lead and some of his toys and took him a mile down the road to the local RSPCA office. I was crying so hard as I walked through the door with him that I didn't wait to offer explanations or complete paperwork, I just threw the lead at them with a bag of Vader's toys,

"I can't look after him anymore, please find him a good home," I hurled over my shoulder as I headed out the door with tears streaming down my face. They shouted something after me, but I just ran. Dick seemed bemused by the decision and distressed by my tears, but he just didn't join up the dots and see that it was down to him.

When I woke the next morning after a night of very little sleep, I could not believe that I had given my dog away, I went back to the RSPCA as soon as I was up, but although it was Saturday, as it was the August bank holiday weekend they were shut. It was a very long three days before I went back to the RSPCA on the Tuesday morning to try to plead my case and get him back. I was sure I could get Dick to be kind to him. I remember standing the other side of the counter as a lady very nicely told me that he had been put to sleep within 30 minutes of being taken in as they had no free kennels and they were about to go into a three-day closure. I hadn't waited for them to explain that they couldn't take him.

The shame of that lives with me to this day, he was a lovely trusting dog who didn't deserve to die because of the mess I had got myself in. I told my parents that I had rehomed him with a nice couple in the countryside. More lies, more shame! I swore never to own a dog again.

Recently, I have signed up to the Dog Trust Freedom Project to foster a dog that has come from someone fleeing from an abusive relationship and so unable to keep them in the short term. Trying to make amends, I guess.

Finally, something good happened. I know, it was all getting a bit bleak wasn't it? In early August I had been called to the Civil Service Interview panel where three very crusty, suited, middle-aged white men, interviewed me across a big wide desk in a government office in Leeds. I think they were impressed by my travel to the States, I was a woman of the world, but most importantly I think, I had passed the IT test. The letter came in early September, declaring me fit to become an Executive

Officer in Her Majesty's Civil Service. Due to the passing of the IT test I was offered a job working in the computer department of the Department of Education and Science up in Darlington. Not quite Customs and Excise and undercover I thought, but reasonably well paid, as at that time people working in Computing, as it was called then, got paid a supplement of about 30% over and above their civil service salary, so I was going to be reasonably well off for the first time in my life.

If only the job had been in London, or somewhere equally far flung, I think that I would have left Dick and Hull and that would have been that. I doubted that Dick would want to go anywhere too far away from Hull. Already in his late 30s he had never left the Northeast, so if it had been in London, I doubt what happened next would have happened. But it was in Darlington; this was 104 miles north of Hull, but it was all on a fast dual carriageway so only took about 90 minutes.

I was definitely going to take the job. I had to get a 'proper' job, one that bore out the university education that the government of the time had so kindly provided for me pretty much free of charge, one that my parents saw as suitable to my position in life and could therefore be discussed with their friends with appropriate pride. I decided that the best plan was to get a flat in Darlington and then commute back and forward to Dick in Hull at the weekends. I can't remember why I made that part of the plan; I think I planned a gradual separation that didn't cause any fuss. That he would stop missing me nd look elsewhere, I would make new friends, sort out real life in Darlington and move on.

But for the first time in my life, I would truly be somewhere where I had no friends, knew no one, so it was a massive step for me. But also, one that I hoped would get me out of the situation I was in, as I planned in a gentle and acceptable way to leave Dick.

We talked about what would happen, how I would go to Darlington and he would stay in Hull and I would see him at the weekends. He realised that I was quite determined to go and so seemed to accept it, times were relatively peaceful.

As autumn started and the nights started to draw in, I went up to Darlington in late September 1984 to start my new job. It became necessary to own a car and so with money I had managed to save whilst living with Dick, I bought a very beat up Hillman Avenger for £250. It was in a lovely bright blue and was a rust bucket as cars in the 80s could be. I could get all of my belongings into it and so moved up to Darlington to start work, taking up residence in the furnished flat that I had found on my reconnoitring visit.

After a few weeks, I realised that Darlington was not working out as my optimistic personality had envisaged, what a surprise. A glittering circle of new girlfriends from work, cosy coffees in town on Saturday morning before a browse through the shops, nights at the cinema, meeting down the pub on a Sunday after a lovely long

walk in the Yorkshire Dales/Moors. Sounds love
doesn't it? I knew this sort of thing happened to othe
people, so why not me? Mostly because I was painfull
and socially inept when left to my own devices, I foun
it hard to initiate relationships with others, particularl
women. I found it hard to put myself out there, and th
opportunities seemed limited too. So two months dowr
the line, I was going to work every day and being botl
lonely and alone during the week, only the weekend:
in Hull seems to be any fun at all, although even tha
didn't last.

The flat I had found was a ground floor flat in a large
converted Victorian three-story house on Stanhope
Road. The road was wide and tree lined and this led me
to believe (wrongly as it happens) that the flats would be
nice and genteel in a shabby chic kind of way (not that
shabby chic was a thing then of course). It really only
turned out to be shabby, but it was the best of the three
I saw on the one day I had ventured up to Darlington
and I liked the location.

We all know these houses, they were and still are
all over the country, three stories high, steps up to the
front door, maybe with pillars either side, massive bay
windows, brick walls at the front with small pineapples
on top each side of the brick pillars at the entrance, a
small lawn and shrubbery the other side of the wall. My
flat was on the ground floor at the front of the house. It
was really only one enormous room, more a bedsit than
a flat then, but the biggest bedsit I had ever seen, my

meagre belongings were lost in it. The new rental TV was lost in one corner. There was a small kitchen and bathroom in what has once been the hall of the house and the bed was in an alcove at the back of the room with a curtain across it. It had impossibly high ceilings and a huge floor-to-ceiling bay window at the front.

I had loved it in September when light flooded in through the bay windows and I slept cocooned and cosy in the alcove bed. I realised I had rushed into things by November when it got cold, there was no central heating, the whole place only had one gas fire in it, and a small electric wall heater in the bathroom. The old sash windows let the wind whistle through them. I spent a long time one afternoon balancing precariously on a table installing DIY double glazing (or plastic sheets with double sided sticky tape) on the massive bay window. The bed in the alcove with the curtain was a god send as I huddled in it night after night reading or watching TV. In its favour, the flat was in a reasonable part of town, with a short walk to the shops.

On the plus side of life, I was loving my work, the first three months involved training to be a computer programmer at the Department of Education and Science offices at Mowden Hall in Darlington.

On site was an older building; The Hall and a four-storey concrete, metal and glass 70s monstrosity housing the majority of the staff, there was also a big computer hall in between the two. Computer programming was a revelation, I felt born to it, the thought processes needed came naturally to me, it was fun, like doing puzzles and solving riddles all day, following the flow of logic to make things happen. This training was all done sitting around a big TV watching instructional videos which six of us watched and then followed up with paper exercises, it went on for 12 weeks, until we were all proficient COBOL programmers. Training completed, I now had a proper job in a proper office with other proper people, I went to the canteen for my lunch at lunchtime, we all went down to The Mowden pub at the bottom of the hill on a Friday lunchtime. These were people who went to work Monday to Friday and did interesting things at the weekend, i.e. anything other than sitting in endless pubs, which I was still doing every weekend when I went back to Hull.

So, what lofty and important work was I doing for the government I hear you ask? Well, I worked on statistical programmes that interrogated all of the data collected from schools and stored on our computers. I worked away on my tiny black screen with green text on it. We provided information to the government on things like the average class size, how many children passed Latin GCSE, child to staff ratios, useful kind of stuff. Our computers also housed and ran the Teacher's Pension Scheme which was probably a lot more important than the stats. I remember once we managed to pay them their lump sums all twice. But the work wasn't the whole picture, I had not made any real friends at work, the other people on my course had all been promoted internally and so already worked at the DES or had come up from the London office to do the training and would leave, I was literally the only new person. Being computing in the 80s, there were an awful lot of bearded men in tank tops and corduroy trousers in the building, you know who you are. There were a couple of other woman in my department, but both were married and a bit older than me, one had a baby and we didn't have much in common.

No one seemed to ever go out anywhere, or if they did, they didn't ask me. I had no idea how to make friends, without even the contact of social media, once you were on your own, you were really on your own. I joined a weekly keep fit class down at the local sports centre on a Monday night. There was a woman from my work there and we both studiously ignored each other apart from a quick nod hello and goodbye.

As my story to date shows, I make 'friends' with men fairly easily, but had not the slightest idea how to make friends with real living women, I was so painfully shy around them. I sat in night after night watching the telly in bed with a blanket around me, eating, sleeping and then doing it all again the next day.

The best times I had was when I belted down the A1 after work on Friday to see everyone in Hull and hang out like before, with people I knew were my friends. I would stay with Dick, play happy families and then get up at 6am on Monday morning to drive back to work.

I still had a foot in each life.

Funnily enough, during this time of commuting, Dick was not violent, maybe he was so grateful to have me home at the weekend, it took the wind from his sails, so to speak. Plus, once I had left Hull, Dick quickly went downhill, he started doing some serious drinking and as a result stopped going to work at all. Serious binge drinking made him quite ill, as he didn't eat, and finally his body just gave up and he had no choice but to sober up.

When he had been working, Monday came around before he could get that bad, but now, Monday was coming and he just kept on drinking, ringing in sick. I supposed luckily for him, he also had quite a bad chest, early emphysema, or COPD as it is now called. Heavy smoking hadn't helped but he had always had a medical weakness in his lungs, they had collapsed twice when he was young, leaving him with quite a lot of scarring which the COPD exacerbated.

I say lucky, as after about two months off work, it was on these grounds, rather than alcoholism that the school and the Department of Education (how ironic) started the process of allowing him to take early medical retirement from teaching on an index linked pension, all before the age of 40. Was he really too sick to work? Well yes he was, but just not for the reason stated. I think it suited both parties, as he had become too unreliable for the school. That all happened slowly, but in the short term, he went onto long-term sickness benefit.

It seemed that despite the way he had treated me in the past, the tables had turned, he needed me now, had become dependent upon me, maybe he even loved me, though it is all still a mystery to me how he really felt about anything.

CHAPTER NINE

Escape avoided

We had a conversation.

"I can't do it anymore," he said to me. He was sad, his head in his hands, fag in hand as always, smoke rising above his bowed head. "I need to be with you, I love you, I miss you, I am going down the toilet here without you."

I knew what was coming, but even then, I was not prepared for it or sure how I felt about it.

"What do you want to do, Dick?" I asked. "I can't come back, I have my new job now."

"I could come to Darlington?" he offered hopefully,

"But you don't know anyone, what will you do all day?" I queried. "What sort of life is that without your friends?"

"They said they would visit." For the first time he

raised his head and looked me in the eye. "We could come back for weekend visits, stay in Paul's spare room."

"You spoke to your friends about this, before me?" I fired angrily at him, but also aware that I mustn't make him angry, so then was suddenly nervous.

"Look, I will think about it, I am not sure it is the right move, give me a week to think about it, OK?" I backtracked.

"OK," he said sadly. He seemed so pathetic and broken and suddenly I held sway over his life, a reversal of roles, me with the power. We went to bed and made love, he was tender and cried afterwards, begging to be allowed to move up to Darlington to live with me.

It's that man-eating tiger again. All I had to say was 'No' and that would have been that. It would have been over, I would have stopped running back to Hull every weekend and got on with my life that was in Darlington. But that is where the problem lay, because as I said, my life in Darlington was not working out the way I had imagined, and loneliness stalked my weekday evenings.

Never once in those three months that I was going back and forth was Dick violent, he was as pathetically pleased to see me as I was him. It was against this backdrop of agreeable living and harmonious relations that when Dick raised the subject of coming up to Darlington to live with me again the following weekend, I did start to give it serious consideration.

Good on me though, I did hold out for a few weeks, but started to feel that the violence was behind us, there was more equality in our relationship, oh and I was lonely, did I say that already? Christmas came and I drove down to Oxfordshire for Christmas and New Year. I think I hoped that Chris might be at home with his parents, but he wasn't. When Christmas was over we took stock.

In January, I helped Dick pack up his flat and sell all his pigeons. He roped in a friend with a works van and he arrived in Darlington with all his worldly possessions to move into my flat/bedsit, which luckily had plenty of room. It all got arranged much as it had been in the flat in Beresford Avenue, so at least I now had a video recorder. We settled down to a rather chilly life, dreaming of the spring. Without his usual pubs to go to Dick settled in and stayed home and painted his metal soldiers, read and watched TV. *Das Boot* was on at the time, which was cheery for me, can't beat a good second world war submarine drama in German with English subtitles. Dick loved anything about the second world war, on which he knew more random facts than anyone else alive, I reckoned.

He kept me company in the evenings, and most importantly, didn't drink. He didn't drink at home unless there was company, and there was definitely no company as we had no friends and so he had no one to go to the pub with. So, it really was behind us. I got the best of Dick; kind, funny, and clever, all to myself. Everything else now seemed like a bad dream.

It is at this point that Dick became John. I know! It was my idea and he just want along with it, a reinvention, a new start, a new name that didn't make people assume he was actually a Dick, it all made sense to me.

CHAPTER TEN

Mortgage anyone?

As we settled down, I realised that the job at the DES in Darlington was my life for the foreseeable future as I built my Civil Service career, and as such, I decided it was time to buy a house.

It was now 1985, the country was not in the best state economically, Mrs Thatcher was not for turning, inflation and unemployment was continuing to rise, and a job was something not everyone could get. So I was lucky to have a very secure and reasonably well paid job. The north was not where I had expected to end up, but it did have the advantage of much cheaper houses than in the south.

With John's iron clad early retirement pension considered, we could get a mortgage with not too many problems, I reasoned. But something also counselled

me against getting a mortgage with John, he wasn't th
great with money, or particularly reliable in many oth
ways too. So sensibly for once, I went to my paren
for a bigger deposit so that I could buy the house i
my sole name. John had been introduced to my paren
on a couple of trips back to Oxfordshire when he wa
always on his best behaviour, but even so, from thei
perspective, he wasn't in uniform, was quite a bit olde
than me and a different class to boot, and so my parent
were not that impressed. My three brothers christened
him 'Pidg' as a result of the pigeon keeping, which i
how they referred to him whenever he was not in the
room.

It is fair to say that my family did not warm to
John. My parents were happy to lend me the money
if it meant that John wasn't on the mortgage, which
given his limited income was sensible and with their
help I could afford the repayments on my salary alone.
My parents also lent me enough to include money to
furnish the house. It took me close to six years to pay
them back, but pay them back I finally did. I found
a little two up two down, front door onto the street,
terrace house, in a cul-de-sac called Herbert Street near
Darlington Station. It had a hallway and a front room
and then another room behind going the full width of
the house with a single storey kitchen extension at the
back with a door out onto the little brick yard. Upstairs
was a double and one single bedroom and a bathroom.

The house was 14 feet wide. The brick yard had an

outside toilet and a gate opening out onto the alley behind. All this was mine for the grand sum of £11,000, and as it was empty I was able to move in quite quickly. I was glad to see the back of the icebox flat, the new house had central heating, amazing!

Herbert Street was quite close to a big old Victorian park called South Park, beds of beautifully arranged flowers in gaudy hews, with winding tarmac paths between large trees and small boating lake and a river winding through it. Also, a Victorian aviary with rather sad birds flitting about in it. Herbert Street also turned out to be by the football ground which could be an issue on a Saturday if you wanted to get anywhere by car, but it was affordable and it was all mine, with John in tow. We got closer and life seemed good. I worked during the day and looked after John and the house at night. There was no violence, and John seemed quite content to stay home and indulge in his hobbies.

This time, nesting and home building was much more exciting as it was my first home, and I bought furniture, carpets and matching kitchen equipment – red and white was in vogue. Despite not working, doing housework and cooking were still not part of John's repertoire when I was around, he was so old-fashioned, or maybe just bone-idle. He painted his metal soldiers, which he was very good at, and using his own pension money built a new pigeon loft in the small brick back yard and bought pigeons to fly again. And he watched whatever daytime

TV was available then which was mostly cricket in the summer and snooker and football in the winter, he was a big fan of all three. He also decided, without consulting me, to get a dog, a Doberman bitch puppy we called Bane (by name and by nature). I was not very happy about this, I had been devastated by what had happened to Vader and did not consider myself a fit person to have a dog, but he just turned up with her one day. I don't even know where she came from, but puppies are very hard to resist and I obligingly fell in love with her.

Typically, I was the one who ended up walking her on long Saturday afternoons in South Park, and looking after her, trying really hard to train her more comprehensively that I had Vader, although I never managed to get her to stop chasing joggers in the park. She would nip at their heels, they were universally terrified, which was very embarrassing. We never did get the hang of the training, Doberman's are known for being very very smart and she was very smart in a sneaky kind of way, that always managed to get the better of us.

I also spent quite a lot of time taking her to the vets as phantom pregnancies were her speciality, but John wouldn't let me get her spayed as he had some idea that she should have puppies at some point. I loved her as best I could, I like to think she loved me back the best. Like me she was a little afraid of John, although he was never violent towards her, as I think he thought she might bite him back, particularly when she was fully grown, I like to think she might have too.

When John moved to Darlington, one good thing I suppose, is that he restarted his relationship with his parents. I say I suppose, as it involved us in a commitment I had not particularly signed up to when I moved, as it required a drive as they lived in the middle of Swale Dale, about 30 miles from Darlington.

I understood that since the exit of his first wife, he had not been to see them as he had never learned to drive and had never owned a car and they were not in the habit of visiting him either. So, we drove down to see them for the first time during the first month in the rented flat, he went for Christmas and then we went every month thereafter, always on a Sunday. They lived much closer to Darlington than Hull, about a 30-minute drive down the A1 past Catterick and then heading over towards Thirsk in a small village called Sinderby with a pub and a shop.

His parents, Don and Nancy, both in their 50s, lived with Nancy's parents – Mary and George who were in their late 70s at this stage. Nancy had retired through ill-health as she had emphysema, which she said had been caused by the inhalation of chemicals at the hairdressers over years and years. Don didn't work either, as far as I could tell he was a feckless man with no talents (oh dear was it so obvious I loathed him from the first time I set eyes on him). Mary, George and Nancy had lived in Stockton on Tees all their lives. George had worked in the steelworks, a very hard but honest life, and John's mother Nancy had worked as a hairdresser for all of hers. Don had been from London originally and had been a merchant seaman and by all accounts not around much when John was growing up, which as it turns out was probably a good thing. John had been raised by his mother and grandparents and I got the impression they had always been one household, whilst Don came and went on the high seas, a lady in every port. John had bucked the trend of his family by going to Teacher Training College and as they say 'making something of himself'.

Between them, they had managed to buy a large retirement bungalow at the end of the village with a big garden and views out over the fields at the back. The four of them had a seemingly harmonious existence, Don went to the pub every lunchtime and most evenings, George gardened and grew prize Chrysanthemums and Nancy and Mary pottered and took care of the house. Nancy struck me as a very sad woman, she rarely laughed or smiled, but breathing was an issue for her and as such she had so little energy, her Mum did the lion's share of the housework and cooking. Don now seemed to cherish the wife he had spent a lot of his life being violent towards. I am not sure what had happened to make him stop but it may have been the risk of losing the only home available to him with Mary and George.

One he stood to inherit in time as he would likely outlive poor Nancy and the pair of them. I know Nancy desperately missed the little girl that John had chosen not to see, but she was brought over the Pennines twice year by her mother for a visit which was nice for them and I was shown all of the photos taken during these visits charting the little girl's life so far. I know it made John sad to see the pictures, but he still believed that no contact was better than limited contact.

On our Sunday visits, John and I would go off to the pub (The Brewers Arms, closed in 1995) for a couple of hours with Don to chew the fat while Nancy and Mary would prepare a Sunday lunch for when we returned. Lunch eaten; tea supped we would head off back up the A1 until the following month. How civilised, how normal, how brain numbingly awful when I look back on it. I gave nothing of myself to any of them. I know that I was snobbish and aloof, going through the motions of a family visit, without caring a great deal. I think going through the motions was a reciprocal thing, as I don't think they really understood what I was doing with John. I was a closed book to them, and them to me.

CHAPTER ELEVEN

Baby Anyone?

Once we were all nicely settled into Herbert Street, I quite quickly got pregnant. I seem to recall we both agreed to do it, although that is probably just me making it all sound a little less contrived on my part. I was 26, no great imperative except I just had a desire, a want, an itch I couldn't scratch. We were settled, happy and it was going to be OK. I got pregnant within one month of coming off the pill. I didn't tell my parents yet, my Nanna (my father's mother) was ill with liver cancer and I knew they did not like John that much, so I decided not to burden them with more bad news.

All was well, I went to work, I read a lot of books about being pregnant. John seemed to mostly ignore that I was pregnant. At 15 weeks pregnant at the end of May, I was already all tummy and felt very pregnant already, nearly halfway, so it was a massive shock, a heart stopping moment when I saw the bright red on the tissue as I wiped myself after going to the loo one morning at work.

'God, I'm miscarrying,' I thought. Fear flooded me; I was going to lose the baby.

I walked gingerly back to my desk, like I was walking on broken glass, if I could have walked with my legs crossed, I would have. My colleagues knew I was pregnant, as I had only just told them. I had not even been at work a full year, so they had not been too impressed I don't think. I made my apologies and drove straight to my GP.

"Of course, a show of blood does not mean you are miscarrying you know."

Know? Of course I knew. I had read every baby and pregnancy book going in the last few weeks. I knew what everything meant, but that didn't stop me being scared witless. Just as well there was no internet then, I would have been a mess of Google Doctor fear and misinformation probably.

"To be on the safe side we'll book you into the General overnight, you can have a scan and then we will know more."

I knew I was just a statistic, as one in three first pregnancies ended in miscarriage, but it was usually much earlier, before 12 weeks. Once I had got past 12 weeks I had assumed it was all going to be OK. I went home to pack a few things and then called a taxi to get to Darlington Memorial Hospital. John had questioned the point of him coming with me as he would have to get a taxi home so he waved me off and said he would come to visit me the next day.

An hour later, I had been booked in and I lay in the Gynaecology ward gazing at the ceiling. A brusque lady doctor had told me to lie completely flat and let things settle down and we would see what the scan said. I was still bleeding and still scared.

I was sharing the ward with three very unfortunate women, my addition made four. Why do I remember them after all this time? I think that I had so little to concentrate on as I lay there trying to keep my baby that I watched and learned a little like I was watching a TV programme. We were a happy crew. The woman opposite had cancer of the ovaries and was in for radiation treatment. The women on her right threw up constantly due to some pregnancy complication, she was wretched (excuse the pun). The girl on my left barely out of her teens was having her third termination followed by sterilisation, which made me quite sad.

In the morning, I went down in a wheelchair for a scan. The two radiologist nurses who did the scan said nothing, just gazed at the monitor, which was turned from me so that I couldn't see it.

The words "Is the baby dead?" screamed into the silence filling the small room, but I didn't ask it. I don't suppose they would have answered anyway. The fact that they didn't smile and show me the ghostly image of my baby, heart pumping away was answer enough.

I was taken back up to my room, and I lay on my back for another 48 hours. No doctor visited me, and no one told me the result of the scan and I was too scared to ask. It seems a cruel thing now, but maybe it was the weekend and there was no one senior enough to break the bad news? I was still bleeding and was now passing small clots. John came to visited me on each of the 3 days I was there. He didn't seem worried and didn't stay long. Finally, on the third day I knew that there was no point in staying any longer. I told the junior doctor on the ward that I was checking myself out. He made a big deal about it being against doctors' advice and that anything that happened would be my fault.

"I need to get this over with one way or another," I said. "If staying pregnant means I have to lie on my back for the next 5 months, then I can't do it, so I am going home to see what happens."

I called another taxi and went home. I was relieved to be home. John was relieved I was home. It was business as usual. I went out to the shops for food, washed, cleaned and cooked tea. Apart from the blood all seemed quiet in the tummy department. In the early evening I lay on the sofa and that's when the crippling pains started. I knew I was going to lose the baby, but I had imagined it would just be like wetting myself. Going into labour was a surprise. If I had thought about it a little it would have made sense. I was 15 weeks pregnant; my baby

as 4 inches long and according to the books, perfectly
rmed. It was not going to just fall out by itself. John
y on the sofa and watched a football match as I lay
1d clutched my stomach and wished it were all over.
ach contraction was like the worst period pain ever
1ultiplied by ten. They got closer and closer and I
idn't think I could take any more. I decided to have a
1ot bath. Upstairs I knelt in the hot water and swayed
)ackward and forward, it really helped. Suddenly, there
was a sort of a whoosh; I felt the baby come out and
:he bath turned pink. I didn't want to look and so just
stayed there for a little not moving. I didn't call John;
I needed to find out for myself first. The thought of
scooping a fully formed four-inch baby from the bath
water was filling me with dread.

Finally, I felt around beneath me and raised my baby
up in my cupped hands. As the water drained away, relief
filled me, followed quickly by sadness. My baby wasn't a
baby after all, it was never meant to be born. Although
it was quite a late miscarriage, most of which happen
before 12 weeks, just like the books said, nature was just
taking care of what would never be. It was about four
inches long, but there the resemblance to a fully formed
baby ended. There were no arms, legs or head. It was a
nice pink colour though with dark spots on each side
where eyes would have been. A large Walls pork sausage
was one description which fitted perfectly.

I sat in the cooling bath water, holding my baby
getting more and more angry at the hospital for letting

me go through this. They must have known after the scan that the baby wasn't going to be born. They should have given me a D and C straight away. If I could have maintained that anger, I might have done something; wrote a letter, complained, but as the water drained from the bath leaving me with the tricky problem of poking the little bits of placenta down the plughole, the anger drained away with it. I was just tired, very very tired and very very sad.

My GP very kindly came out and checked over me and my baby. He seemed embarrassed by having to examine the baby, rather distasteful for a GP.

"Never mind, looks like it was for the best, this is a bit of a cliché I know, but you're young and healthy, you can try again, but maybe wait for six months for your body to get back to normal first."

Kind words, what a sterling chap. "Porky" lay where I had left him, on some toilet paper on top of the cistern. "Porky" had become a 'he' when his father christened him having finally come to see him; after all he was far too ugly to be a girl. John and I found ourselves giggling hysterically as we came up with more and more outlandish scenarios for if our sausage had lived. I think I was just relieved it was all over, and the sausage jokes were born more of mild hysteria than any kind of cruelty. I know I fully realised the awfulness of it all, but just didn't want to admit it.

What to do with the baby became a problem to me over the next 24 hours. I couldn't bring myself to put him in the bin, and with no garden a burial was also not possible, so as he shrivelled, obviously, I couldn't keep him. Finally, with a quick "Goodbye!" he went down the toilet. As the water flushed, I regretted it immediately. I should have buried him, I imagined myself at dead of night burying him in the park and getting caught.

"Hello, Hello, what have we 'ere?"

"Just burying my dead baby, Officer. Will you join me in a prayer?"

Or worse, he might have been dug up again by a dog and traumatised the poor owner, or maybe not, they would just think it was a sausage.

So, down the toilet he went, life can be very cruel indeed sometimes. Possibly if I had thought about it, maybe the ethereal being up there was trying to tell me that having a child with this man was not a good idea, for me or the child. Remember how good I was at listening to advice? Particularly from a nebulous being I didn't even believe in. The cheek of it, trying to tell me what to do.

The day after, I finally phoned my parents and told them I had been in hospital for three days and why, so they learnt of their prospective grandparenthood and lack of it in the same sentence. I don't think that I ever managed to convince my mother I had a miscarriage, she assumed that I'd had an abortion and was just covering it up by calling it a miscarriage. This version made sense to her, as she didn't like John and we weren't married at the time. My dad said not a word about it at all – women's business.

For a couple of years after, my mum would occasionally pipe up saying, "How old would your baby be now?", "Do you think it was a boy or a girl?", "Do you ever wish you had kept it?". Things that showed her complete lack of understanding of what had happened and the impact it had on me and that I'd not had a choice about keeping it. Miscarriage is handled a little more sympathetically these days, but it is still seen as a very private thing and not good form to discuss too much, just get on with trying again seems to be the mantra.

I do know now that you need some sort of mental support and I didn't get it from anyone. My mother in particular had made up her own story to fit the narrative and just didn't seem to understand how to support me, which made me doubly sad and still does. I was very tired physically for about three months afterwards, everything seemed an effort and I took no joy in anything at all. Again, no one told me what to expect or what was normal or not, but I suspect I had post-natal depression driven by haywire hormones.

Years later, a woman I knew at work miscarried her baby. Everyone tiptoed around not knowing what to say. I gave her a card saying how sorry I was for her and her husband's loss, she was so grateful that her missing child was being acknowledged, but it seemed the least I could do.

CHAPTER TWELVE
Lodgers and Dodgers

It was the strangest thing, but not long after my miscarriage, Gary from the Hull crew came to live in our spare room. Like a lot of things that happened at that time, I am not sure how it came about exactly, some incident or another around his broken family meant he had to get out of Hull.

He didn't have any ties or a job and he was living in a bedsit, so asked if he could come to Darlington and lodge with us for a while. The spare room was tiny, but I figured that it would give John company and might be just the thing for me too as Gary had given up drinking a while back and was going to AA at the time and we would get a little bit of extra income from the DSS rent payments he received. Either way it seemed to me a win-win.

When I was in the early stages of my pregnancy, I had held off decorating the small room for the baby so it was still a blank magnolia canvas. We bought a single bed and a chest of drawers and he moved in. I found out that as he wasn't working he was happy to clean and cook every day which was kind of nice for me. He loved to walk Bane too, and I think it is him that she ended up loving the most, she certainly took to sleeping in his room with him.

Now fully grown, she was a big scary-looking dog, he got her a studded leather collar and a very short chain lead, and he would walk around the surrounding streets in a t-shirt to show off his muscles as he had also gone on a keep fit crusade as well, doing a lot of weight training. Also, even though John continued to be on his best behaviour and there had been no 'incidents' for a long time, I thought that having another person in the house would stop him getting violent, which worked for me too. So win-win-win.

Gary did start to job hunt once he got to Darlington, but this was the 80s and unemployment was through the roof, jobs for people in their late 30s with no obvious qualifications were hard to come by. In the meantime, he lived off DSS payments and all was peaceful and harmonious in our now little household of three, plus the dog and some pigeons. The next few months went by without anything much out of the ordinary happening.

Thinking back now, sharing my home with someone who engaged with me, helped me and was good company

ade it a much happier home and should really have
ointed to the fact that John was not actually that good
ompany or support in comparison.

izarrely to me on reflection now, John and I decided
o get married before trying for another baby. I don't
emember a proposal, maybe we just talked about it in a
okey way, as we often approached difficult subjects and
ecisions. But somehow it became fact. There definitely
wasn't a ring of any kind but it was agreed and so in June
of 1985 I started to organise the wedding which was to
oe in August.

Me and that stripey feline, we really were the best of
friends. He just gave me a little nip now and again to
remind me that I really didn't have a clue what I was
doing, or why I was doing it.

All was going well, Darlington John as opposed to
Hull Dick was someone that I could love and get along
with, he was good company and we were a well-formed
unit now. The violence really did seem to be behind us,
and I was much more relaxed. A small wedding was
planned for August at the Registry Office, with a small
low-key reception after. Some of my family were coming,
my mum and dad and my eldest brother, John's mum
and dad and grandparents and the crowd from Hull.
Sean was to be best man, and Gary was helping me out
with all the arrangements. I didn't have any girlfriends
so there was no hen party and no bridesmaids or Maid
of Honour.

Three weeks before the wedding, my Nanna died. She was 87 and I was not very sad as she had been quite ill for a few months, but it was very hard on my dad who was an only child. I went to the funeral down in Ilkeston with the rest of my family and returned the next day. John didn't come with me, as I have said before, travelling away from home was not something he was very keen on and he had finally started to understand that my parents were not that keen on him.

After the funeral, we all went back to my Nanna's sheltered housing flat that she had lived in for the last two years of her life. She had spent most of her life living in her family home, a two-up, two-down terraced house in Ilkeston, the one my father had been born and raised in, not that dissimilar to the one I was living in now. She had raised my father with the help of her spinster sister Annie. My dad had been the result of a love affair which had ended and she had never married, this was a rare thing indeed in 1928, she had been able to do this as her father had supported her as an unmarried mother, and she had kept my dad and remained in her family home. As I said, a remarkable woman.

My dad helped me to sort out some of her things that he thought I might like or indeed need for my house, some china and kitchen stuff (which I did need) jewellery (not my style but sentimental) and her old singer sewing machine (I could sew when I put my mind to it having done an O' level in Needlework, grade 6), a pencil drawing of a horse that I had done and she had framed (I am no artist, but it was nice to have it back), an oak bookcase that my father's uncle Albert had made (I had started to accumulate a lot of books), I still have the bookcase in my hallway now. We packed them into my car with difficulty, and I took them back up the M1 and the M18, as mementos and memories of an amazing lady.

It had been a long and sad couple of days, and I was tired and fractious when I got back. I returned to find John raging drunk. As I had been away, he had decided to go to the pub for once. Without thinking it through due to being tired I guess, I asked him despite the state he was in, if he could help me unload the car as Gary was out. All of the things I had brought back really annoyed John for some reason, or maybe he was going to be annoyed whatever I did. He called me a grave robber and a ghoul, and as I came back through the front door with the last few items, he stood in my way and as I tried to squeeze by him in the tiny hall, he hit me hard. He blacked my eye.

It had been such a long time, over a year since he had done something like this, that yet again I found myself in a state of disbelief, of shock and with no real plan of what to do next. I went to the kitchen and got some frozen peas out of the small freezer compartment in the fridge and held it to my eye for a while as I contemplated what to do next. John was already back in front of the Radio Rentals TV, so I went upstairs and went to bed.

I thought about what I would say to everyone at work – "I walked into a door" seemed to work, makeup was applied to hide the bruising and I wondered if the bruising would be gone before our wedding in less than two weeks. Believe me when I say that I did think about cancelling the wedding and throwing him out, but I didn't. Hope springs eternal and I decided it was a one-off, definitely a one-off, and sure enough the peace that was restored the next day would last for nearly another year.

We actually had quite a nice wedding, helped in some small part by lovely sunny weather. I have the pictures, I know that the shadow of a bruise is still there under my eye, but no one else could see it, or that there was a small shadow of sadness about me. I can see it now in the pictures, but I didn't feel it at the time, maybe I was still a little numb. The August sunshine shone on us, my mother's face was perfect. I don't think she thought she had anything to smile about, but she was there with my dad, which I appreciated. My eldest brother and father were both in good form, charming the women present, I look pretty, thin and nervy in the pictures, dressed in a white broderie anglaise dress with a blue sash with a flower in my hair. All the old crew from Hull were there, Sean made a perfect best man. Linda was pregnant with their first child and so had not accompanied him.

We all met up at the Registry Office in the town. We all went together as John had not decamped elsewhere the night before as is traditionally done. John's parents and his grandfather George had driven up. John's grandmother had died, and George was still quite overcome by it all, they had been married for 60 years and he was lost without her. Nancy was frail and as quiet as a mouse as was usual and I'm not sure she and my mother had a lot to say to each other. My mother was not one for small talk with people she didn't know and Nancy was shy. On reflection, maybe my mother was shy too, certainly ill at ease.

The ceremony was short and my name was changed and John now owned half of everything I had worked so hard for. This did worry me a little bit I have to admit, but this is all with the benefit of hindsight. On the day I was happy and I enjoyed it. We had a wedding breakfast in the Station Hotel up the road from Herbert Street. It was a Victorian Hotel, we were in a large function room with swirly carpets, big dusty windows and red velvet seating. The forty of us were lost in it. Barely edible ham salad, followed by trifle was swilled down with lots of lager. The budget was meagre, and no help had been offered from either sets of parents, although to be fair, I hadn't asked. I know we received presents but I have no recollection of what they were. I think I asked for vouchers for one of the catalogues at the time – Littlewoods quite likely, so I could buy matching sheets and blankets and towels, rather than the mismatched lot that had spewed forth from my mother's very capacious airing cupboard when I had first moved into the house.

The wedding was nothing like my first wedding

to Tom in the Officer's Mess. No morning suits or champagne or hats, or long-lost friends of my parents that I had never even met. Chris was not there to tell me it should have been him. Where was he? Damn him, how I missed him, but he was still living out his sentence in Algeria. But despite that, it all went off swimmingly as they say in not so leafy Oxfordshire. I realised that there was only one person from Darlington at the wedding; my next-door neighbour, a single mum who Gary was trying to get to go out with him and she came as his plus one.

So, that was how good I had been at making friends. I didn't invite my colleagues at work, I think I was too embarrassed and ashamed by the size of the wedding and the venue. What kind of snob was I? You just can't take the middle class out of the girl I guess. My mother's face just reinforced that feeling, and makes me reflect less positively about the day as I remember it. The pictures say that a happy time was had by thirty-nine of us at least. About twenty of us went back to our little house afterwards. John's family headed back down the A1 and mine to the hotel they were staying in. The Hull contingent had all come on the train so eventually they too all sloped off to catch the last train back and the day was called to a close, with me, Gary and the next-door neighbour tidying up the debris.

As is often the case in my recollection, I have no idea what John was doing after it nor can I recall if he seemed happy or not.

CHAPTER THIRTEEN

A Real Baby

I was pregnant again by September, and for the next few months while we waited for the baby to come, I went to work, John looked after his pigeons and watched TV and Gary walked Bane, cooked and cleaned and looked for work.

I was very happy, I couldn't wait to have the baby, it was the only thing that mattered now. After the miscarriage I fretted badly for the first four months of my pregnancy, I read pregnancy book after pregnancy book again, I must have owned ten of them. I nagged the doctor for extra scans to see if everything was all right in the first four months. Every time I went to the loo I gazed into the bowl and into my knickers for the tell-tale flash of red. But I had the grainy little picture I was given at my first scan, showing a baby with arms and legs, a head and a heartbeat and I was reassured.

As I passed 16 weeks, I settled down and believe the baby would be born healthy. I started to we horrendous corduroy pinafore smocks, which seeme to be the only pregnancy clothes you could buy the I put jumpers under them in the winter and then spring came, blouses with full sleeves, long cuffs an pointy collars become the order of the day. I do no have a single picture of me pregnant, although to b honest, apart from my wedding, I have very few picture of when I lived in Darlington. Maybe I put my littl Olympus Trip camera away and just didn't get it ou again until the baby came.

Thankfully, for the whole nine months all was quiet and peaceful on the John front, I got bigger and bigger and life was good. John obviously had a code of conduct that wouldn't let him hit a pregnant woman. We all agreed that our strange little menage a trois had to come to an end and that Gary needed to move out in time for me to decorate the little room. Well I say me, Gary agreed to do it and he painted it a lovely lemon yellow colour. I did know by then what sex my baby was, I was having a boy, but my mother didn't want to know, so at least the lemon yellow was not going to give anything away, not that she visited during my pregnancy. Although I must have gone down there at some time in that nine months to see them as I already had the secondhand wooden cot that my Mum picked up from a friend who had run out of new grandchildren.

I got a new mattress for it and popped it in the corner of the little lemon-yellow room. I had a small white flatpack chest of drawers that doubled as a changing table. The flatpack drawers were rickety and flimsy despite our best efforts in screwing and gluing. No IKEA to call upon in those days. Bright yellow curtains with teddy bears on hung at the small window overlooking the brick yard. A cardboard mobile of cut out teddies floated and twirled above the cot. I found myself spending more time in there, folding and refolding the tiny clothes, bought after hours of browsing in Mothercare, packed neatly away in the chest of drawers.

Although my mother didn't want to know the sex of her first grandchild, she continually asked me what colour of matinee jackets to knit, so I opted for yellow and white so as not to give her any clues. This was her first grandchild and she was knitting for England. I think I ended up with about 25 jumpers and matinee jackets, most of them for a baby up to six months and he was due in June, so he would outgrow them before he needed them. But she was happy, so I said thank you and put them in the little chest of drawers. I still have a lot of them, although I finally parted with some recently to go to Ukraine, and some to my first grandchild too. The rest remain, unworn and anachronistic, but oh so sweet to get out and look at when I am feeling nostalgic.

Gary did not go far when he moved out luckily; I think

he would have missed Bane and her him. He moved to the end of the street near to South Park to lodge with a single lady who immediately hit on him, but it was not reciprocated, so he spent a lot of time hiding in his room to avoid her attentions. His closeness did mean that he could still visit regularly and come and walk Bane a couple of times a day so that was one less thing for me to worry myself about.

I went to work every day and planned for the baby at night. As I was the main source of our income, I would have to return to work as soon as I could. Even though it was a gold-plated civil service job, I had been working there less than two years, so I only got 12 weeks paid maternity leave, and with no savings, there were no options to extend this. John was going to look after the baby once I went back to work.

I know, I know, please don't shout at the book. John was calm, sober and nice, and although he took little interest in my pregnancy, he was planning to be daddy of the year. I left the books out for him and he reminded me that he has gone through one pregnancy and labour and had one child already.

I stopped work about two weeks before my due date. Given my maternity leave, I really wanted the baby to come on time or even a little bit early, but no such luck. The weather that June was exceptional – well for the 80s, not so much now I guess. I was extremely uncomfortable with temperatures into the high 20s. It was a big relief when I finally went into labour in the afternoon of June 27th about six days past my due date. The very hot weather had been exhausting, but finally we were on the way. After a few hours walking around at home and knowing I had to get a taxi, I decided I needed to go to the hospital, but I waited as long as I could bear it. Finally, I stopped striding about the house and leaning on walls when the contractions came and at about 8pm I phoned for a taxi and I headed off to the hospital. I didn't tell the taxi driver I was in labour in case he wouldn't take me or panicked, and I managed to make the short journey in uncomfortable silence.

John said for them to ring him once it was getting nearer and he would come. Once installed on the labour ward on my back and hooked up to various monitors, I pretty much laboured alone in a bed for about the next 5 hours. Midwives were a bit thin on the ground and there were horrible noises of other woman in labour all around me. Not even my miscarriage prepared me for the pain, which was similar but about 10 times worse. Spoiler alert to all those first-time pregnant ladies out there, natural child birth is very painful, but I won't go on about that anymore, except to say every pain is worth it.

Finally, a midwife checked on me and decided I was getting close enough and I was wheeled into another room to get ready for delivery and closer monitoring. They thought I was going to be another two hours probably and finally gave me some Pethidine for the pain and called John to come. He arrived by taxi at two in the morning just in in time to hold my hand for the last two minutes of labour, as the predicted two hours turned out to be 45 minutes. As he came into the delivery suite, I was horrified to realise he was drunk. It was the first time in nine months, he must have gone out to the pub. I wish he hadn't bothered to come; he reeked of alcohol and was swaying on his feet. I had been scared and alone for five hours, but remember very little of the final 45 minutes due to the Pethidine. I do know that John passed out at the appropriate moment of me pushing out the head as it was very hot in the delivery room, so he missed the final moments and caused a big distraction.

As a result in the process of crowning (what kind of expression is that anyway? It makes it sound quite nice, it isn't!) I suffered what I would politely call a bad vaginal injury and the midwifes called a 'graze' that they said didn't need stitching. I don't believe it to this day, although it did heal in time. So where I should have had an episiotomy and some nice neat stiches, I got a bit of labial re-sculpturing instead – nice!

Once I was on a ward with James in a cot next to me, John went back home by taxi and I sat, unable to sleep, gazing at baby James who was perfect. He had a little fat strawberry mark on his thigh and I loved that too. He was a slightly unimpressive 7 pounds and looked like a little skinned rabbit. I stayed up the rest of the night with him, cuddling him and hoping he would

y to breast feed, but he was still very sleepy from the
Pethidine and just slept. I watched the sun come up over
Darlington and felt very blessed to have my son. You
note that I don't say our son. But yes, I think even then
I considered him entirely mine.

James was my parent's first grandchild, born
serendipitously on my father's 59th birthday. My dad
spent his birthday on a four hour dash up the motorways
with my mother, to see me and James (named after my
grandfather on my mum's side). They arrived with John
at about 11am the next morning, so I am guessing they
had not slept either since getting their call from John at
three in the morning. They could not have been more
delighted, and in their company, John finally seemed
very taken with his newborn son.

It all turned to worms a bit over the following few
days for me however, I really wanted to breastfeed as I
believed this was absolutely the best thing for my baby
and also the easiest and cheapest thing too, given that
money was going to be tight with maternity leave. But
James got jaundice as a result of the Pethidine given too
late in my delivery, it is supposed to wear off out your
system before the baby is delivered, but he came out
with Pethidine overdose and was drowsy and jaundiced
and wouldn't latch on. Sadly, I didn't get the support I
needed from the midwives who were very busy, and I
was encouraged to give him bottles as a stop gap and to
try expressing my milk for him. I tried the great breast

pump machine installed in a soulless medical suppl[y] room down the hall, full of bedpans and dressing[s] sitting on a hard chair, pent up and anxious, suffi[ce] to say, my milk stayed resolutely in my breasts, until [I] went back to bed where it dribbled constantly into m[y] nightie. I stayed in hospital for six days due to James['] jaundice, so by the time I got out I was broken of m[y] breast-feeding tendencies and James was a bottle-fe[d] baby and the die was cast. This would come back t[o] haunt me as like a lot of women who try to do the mos[t] natural thing in the world and don't succeed, I felt like [a] failure as a mother before I had even started. My whol[e] hospital birth and breast-feeding experience with Jame[s] led me to have my other two children as homebirths a[s] far away from hospital as possible which was both scary and brilliant and both were quite fanatically breast fed, although not easily to start with but I was on a mission and did finally succeed with both of them.

CHAPTER FOURTEEN

Around We Go Again

By the time James arrived and I got out of hospital, I only had another 9 weeks of my 12 weeks maternity leave left. I was determined to make the most of this precious time together and also to get John into the swing of the daily care of an infant, as that is what we had decided was the best use of his time and our finances. James was doing well on the bottle, starting to sleep a bit at night and generally all was well.

There were challenges. My mother, in her excitement at being a grandmother for the first time, had turned up on her second visit about a week after the first with a huge Silver Cross pram, the wheels were larger than the ones on my car! She had not thought it through sadly, although meant well. Our terraced house had a hallway only three feet wide and that is where the pram, at nearly two feet wide had to reside, but for now we would squeeze past it on our way in and out and I used it to take James up to the park at the end of the road and wheel him around in the fresh air as many a mother before me had done, and he could sleep in it during the day rather than taking him up to his cot. But the main problem with the pram was that it would not go into the car without being taken apart, so it was only an amount of appropriate time before it went to the second-hand shop and I got a normal sized pushchair that his car seat would clip into. This car to pushchair combo was the height of baby car seat engineering for the day, when it was not even compulsory to have a car seat for a baby, as baby car seats were a fairly new-fangled invention.

Luckily, Bane had taken to James, which was a relief. She took an interest in him but nothing that worried us, but of course we never left them together, which was an additional burden of care that I needed to impress upon John before I went back to work. So, there we were, trotting along quite nicely, week six of James's life, three weeks before going back to work, when it all went wrong again. John's ex-wife contacted him. He was still paying her £25 a month in maintenance payments for the little girl, now almost seven years old, and so they had each other's details. She had recently got re-married and her new husband wanted to adopt the little girl before they had another child together. Even though he didn't see her, it was obvious that John loved his little girl. He'd had a whole year with her as a baby and despite the time that had passed since then, he was finding this news hard to absorb and then to decide about. He had never wanted to see her and yet giving her up was a different thing, she would not have his name anymore, she would be completely detached from him. I suspect that the ex-wife felt that she had a better chance of him agreeing now that he had re-married and had James.

She sent a picture the little girl had drawn showing the husband as her Daddy with them holding hands, it was what she wanted, to have this man's name as he was the only Daddy she had ever known, and she had no memory of John. After a few days of soul searching he did finally agree and sign the paperwork. He gave a condition that the little girl should continue to be taken to see her grandparents in Sindersby twice a year and this was agreed, although I suspect that his ex would have done this anyway, she was a good person by all accounts. The whole thing seemed to break him, put him on edge, it rocked his equilibrium, it rocked his world and I think contributed to what happened next.

Since James had been born and I had been at home all day, John had taken to occasionally going to the pub at lunch-time, mostly on the weekends, nothing bad, I thought, it all seemed under control and I wasn't worried about it. I think having a baby in the house meant he thought he needed a break from being a father. But one Sunday lunchtime he didn't come back. I found out later that he been taken to a working men's club by someone he had befriended in the pub, so the drinking had continued until about five that afternoon.

When he came back, I was in the front room with James getting ready to put him down for a nap in his pram in the hallway. John came into the front room. We started to row, or I did anyway, I had cooked Sunday lunch expecting him back at 2pm and I was justifiably pissed off with him. Oh, what a short memory I had. I was standing on one side of the small front room with James still in my arms and John on the other, I gave him a piece of my mind. I had forgotten, you see. The safe behaviour put aside, he was out of order, I spoke my mind, about responsibility, about thinking of others, about caring for his son, about how he couldn't do things like this anymore.

John had taken up golf since we came to Darlington. He had bought a small second-hand set and he went to the local municipal course for 9 holes every so often at the weekends. His golf clubs were in the corner of the front room, While I was berating him, he pulled one out of the golf bag (I found out later, it was one of the woods), I saw what he was doing and stopped berating him and just stood very still. He came towards me very slowly, the room was small, this didn't take more than two strides. there was no time for me to react, to assimilate what was happening. I saw it then, murder was in his eyes, plain and simple, this was not like the other times, I truly believed in that moment that he was going to kill me. He put himself at just the right distance

om me and swung at my head just once with the golf
ıb with all the force he could manage while shouting
ıe word "Enough!"

I still had James in my arms and some sort of
reservation instinct kicked in, if not for myself then
or my child and I managed to duck as the club whistled
owards my head. He missed us both and took a chunk
ut of the wall behind me, snapping the shaft of the
lub with the force of the impact. I truly believe it would
ave killed me if it had connected with my head.

While John was stumbling around trying to pick up
he remains of the golf club, I dodged past him pushed
vast the pram and ran out the front door with James as
f the hounds of hell were behind me, which I guess in
some way they were.

I ran up the road to the house that Gary was now
lodging in as fast as I could. It wasn't far, which was
just as well. It was August, so it was warm, but we had
left as we were, me in my slippers, James in a babygro.
No money, nothing for James in terms of sustenance. I
hoped Gary was in, he was still the only person I really
knew in Darlington that I could go too, John did not
follow me, I only found out why later.

When I arrived, the lady Gary lived with let me in
and the three of us congregated in her living room
while I told them through tears and shaking what had
happened. She tried to get me to ring the police, I was
not keen, but she insisted and so finally I did. This was

the first time I had admitted my situation to anyo[ne]
other than Gary.

The police said they would go around to the hous[e]
find John and let me know what the situation wa[s]
we were to wait there until they contacted us. It w[as]
Sunday, the shops were shut (Yes completely shut,
know, nothing, not even a petrol station. No food [or]
drink to be bought anywhere for miles.) I had no bab[y]
milk or any nappies for James, I had no money, no ca[r]
keys or house keys. James had been due a bottle after hi[s]
nap which had not happened, so he was both tired an[d]
hungry and was crying bitterly.

The three of us made an attempt to feed him wit[h]
watered down tinned carnation milk on a spoon whic[h]
was less than successful. He did finally fall into a[n]
exhausted sleep on the sofa.

After a couple of hours, I had still not heard anything
from the police, and I realised that eventually I was going
to have to go back home. If John was there, hopefully
the police would manage him while I got my things,
got the car and maybe went down to my parents. (I
sometimes wish this is what had happened as it would
have brought everything to a close, but that's not how it
panned out.) The police did finally ring to say that John
was no longer in our house, his father had come up to
get him and taken him away, the house was safe for me
to return too and that an officer would wait there to let
me in.

Me, James and Gary set off up the road back home,

it was now dark and I was glad that Gary was with me, although didn't really want him to have to get involved with John. They were friends and it didn't seem right that he had to take sides.

When we got to the house the policeman told me that when the golf club had broken, as I was running for the door, the sharp metal shaft end had bounced up and cut John's wrist really badly. He was bleeding so much; he had had to call 999. Before taking him to hospital, the ambulance crew that came for him had seen the house, seen the signs of a baby and blood everywhere and called in the police at about the same time that I had. This turned out to work in my favour in the future, as John never knew that I had rung them as well.

As I walked in, our house looked like a murder scene where John had trailed around the house dripping blood into every room, up and down stairs while he drunkenly decided what to do. It took me many hours on my hands and knees to scrub it all out of the carpets, which luckily were a fetching shade of blush pink to start with.

When John had come back from the hospital to find the police at the scene, it had been decided that he should not stay in the house as I needed to come back, the police rang Don, and he had driven up to collect him and take him back to their house.

After that, it was just me and James for the next two weeks. John rang most nights asking to come home and I kept saying no, but I was running out of options. I was due back to work, and had asked for an extra week maternity leave without pay while I tried to decide what to do as I had no childcare for James.

The police had talked to me about pressing charges, but although badly frightened, we had not been hurt, and it all seemed to fade away like the blood scrubbed from the carpets. I suspect that the childbirth memory wipe was wiping other memories at the same time. I let the gentle fog of amnesia wash over me, cleansing me from making a decision. Pressing charges was the end of our marriage and our family and I wanted to try to keep it going, I wanted to try to fix it and make it better, I wanted James to have a father. I just failed to see what was in front of me, or blindly refused to acknowledge that it was not ever going to be the way I wanted or hoped. I told my own family and work nothing at all about any of it. Secrets bind you to someone, and I was binding myself even tighter to John in my future. I fantasised about how it could be if John went back to sobriety again. I told the police that I didn't want to press charges and nothing more was said.

Don drove John home two weeks after he had picked him up, his wrist was still bandaged, it seems he had lost a lot of blood and the injury had been quite serious. Don told me rather grandly that John would never repeat this behaviour, they had spent many an hour discussing the ramifications. John's mother had also sat him down for a heart to heart, how she couldn't bear it to lose another grandchild, how I was the best thing since sliced bread and certainly the best thing that had happened to him since his first wife left him. John seemed to have taken all of this on board and understood that he would lose everything if he didn't change his ways. The icing on the cake was Don promising to personally come up and beat the living daylights out of him if he transgressed again. I believed the last bit; it was what Don had been doing to people all his life.

I am not sure he saw the irony in all of it, threatening violent behaviour with more violent behaviour, behaviour that John had learnt from him in the first place! The irony was not lost on me however, but John was very contrite yet again, making all sorts of promises, crying as he held James and me again.

CHAPTER FIFTEEN

Another House, Only Bigger

We quickly settled back into a sober routine, and a week later I had to go back to work. Leaving James that first morning was very very hard, particularly in light of what had only just happened, leaving him with John was a huge leap of faith. My work colleagues were very kind and welcomed me back with cake and some sympathy for leaving such a young baby. I was saved from too much misery by pragmatism and recognising that I didn't have the luxury of choice. It helped that I really enjoyed my work and by the end of the day I was all caught up with what I had missed, knew what we had planned for the next couple of months and couldn't wait to get stuck in. My brain engaged, my interest peaked, purpose and routine in my life. This I realise now has always been my stay, my safety, my solace, to be busy, needed, useful. Bring it on!

When I got home that first day without seeing my son every hour of his day, without knowing when he had slept, how much he had eaten, how many nappies he had soiled, what noises and faces he had made, it seemed that all was well. It seemed that way because it was that way. James was in his little bouncy chair on the living room floor with John watching cricket on the telly. He was fed and dry and nothing bad had happened.

I got on with cooking the tea and catching up on housework, and then I got to spend some precious time with James, feeding him, bathing him and putting him to bed. And so we went on, all settled again and going along nicely. And that is how it stayed for the next few months. When I think on it now, we were a strange family, we never went anywhere together except to our respective parents, we didn't go out for meals or to the pub anymore. I would go alone to walk James and Bane in the park. Gary, our only friend, would visit, sometimes walk with me, sometimes watch the cricket with John. We never once considered going on holiday. It might be that there was just not the money for it or just that John didn't like to travel, but our only entertainment was each other and television.

We went to my parents for Christmas 1986. All my brothers were there, it was a happy houseful, and my parents were polite to John and he was on his best behaviour. James was five months old, and I have videos that my dad took, hours and hours of James being passed around everyone and getting help opening all the presents my Mum had bought for her first grandchild's first christmas. He was spoilt rotten, he had never had so much attention, his three uncles and his grandparents were all very enamoured, and why should they not be, he was a smiley, engaging, gurgling, happy little baby, and I had a nice rest. At some point in his first five months, James had become Jamie, I liked the softness of this version of his name.

In the new year, I got a pay rise at work. These happened as regular as clockwork in the Civil Service then and I was in an occupation that was considered to be specialist, so once my years' probation had finished I had gone up a pay scale and my £6k a year salary had jumped up to £10K and as I passed my second year anniversary it jumped up again.

We had been in Herbert Street for nearly two years, and I started to consider a bigger house with a garden for Jamie. He was starting to take a lot more interest in his surroundings and as John never took him to playgroups or the park, he was not getting enough stimulation I thought. Having a garden at about the time he started toddling would work quite well, I thought.

All the DIY would keep John busy as well. I thought it would mean we could finally get rid of the pigeon loft and pigeons in our back yard. As usual, John had not been racing them and they were just pets and a drain on our limited resources, as well as being messy, smelly and noisy. Also, it would be good for Bane to have a garden too. Gary was still very kindly walking her twice a day and I think if he had been able to, he would have offered to take her, but for now she got the exercise she needed. I thought it would put all the bad memories associated with the house behind us.

In order to qualify for an increased mortgage, I would have to make it a joint one and put John's name on the mortgage and get his pension taken into account, but it seemed possible. I was full of hope and possibilities and so I started to house hunt. This action epitomises my optimistic and hopeful nature, that said, I thought that the bad times were well and truly behind me. We were a nice, happy, normal family and we were going to move to a new house. Me thinks I thunk to much.

I found a house in a suburb called Cockerton to the southwest of Darlington, not far from the A1 as it whistled past the town. John seemed happy enough for me to house hunt and just take him to the final short list, which ended up having just one house on it.

It was in Crossfields Road. It was an unprepossessing red brick semi-detached house. Not one of those grand ones you see in avenue after avenue in the south, with fake Tudor timbers and elaborate brick work and large curved bay window with a garage attached and large sweeping front gardens. No, it had none of those things. It was small with the rectangular bay window sticking out somewhat uncomfortably from the front of the house looking like it has been stuck on, all angles rather than curves. The garage was detached and set back from the house down a rough concrete drive. It had almost three bedrooms: a double and two singles. But it was bigger than our current house and it had a long garden and a lovely sunny eat-in kitchen at the back with french doors on to the garden.

The front garden was a small lawn and shrubbery and a rather un-flattering wall made of breeze blocks with holes cut out of them to make a pattern. The back garden consisted of a few paving slabs calling themselves a patio outside the french doors, a concrete path running top to bottom with a washing line strung on two poles either end. There was a single apple tree of some size and tussocky grass for the rest, no flowers or shrubs, small wire fences on either side leaving me a bit exposed to the neighbours. But for a lot of the reasons shown in the description, we could afford it. It was also in a cul-de-sac with an old railway line at the top of the cul-de-sac that Bane could be walked along in the evening. It was also only a ten minute drive to work.

We moved in in March 1987. Herbert street had sold fairly quickly, and I had made a small profit due to my tasteful improvement of the interior décor (I kid you not!). Crossfields Road was over twice the price I had paid for Herbert Street, but this was the 80s. Inflation and house prices were running wild, it was now or never, it was a done deal. The small profit I made on Herbert Street was enough to cover the larger deposit and the stamp duty, so I went from having a £11,000 mortgage to having one for £23,000. It was a massive leap and it meant we might struggle a little until my next to be expected pay rise.

The sale went though, our meagre belongings were moved in. We owned most of what we needed already. We still rented our TV but we thought we might splash out and buy our own once we had moved in. We did the lot with a van and three runs back and forth with Gary helping. The only new thing we needed was a table and chairs for our sunny kitchen diner, which I think I bought on the never-never from Argos. Oh, and a lawn mower, our new neighbour sold me an old one of his for very little, I think he was glad to see the mess of a garden tidied up.

I was quite happy playing housy-housy again for a while, painting the big red brick fireplace in the back room white, and the acres of anaglypta wall paper a lighter shade other than magnolia. The sofa was parked in the living room bay window, Bane loved standing on it and barking at all the passersby on the street. I put up some net curtains at the front windows and also started making some new curtains for the living room on my Nanna's old Singer.

CHAPTER SIXTEEN

Settling into a Quiet Life

enjoyed not having to commute through the town traffic to get to work, it had been a fairly short commute before but this one was even shorter, on easier roads and much less stressful. I could even pop home at lunchtime if I needed to. As predicted, John was happy to get on with sorting the garden and redecorating the house, alongside caring for the baby.

In the garden, the main job being to tame the tussocky grass back into something that looked like a lawn, although he also dug up the top of the garden and called it a vegetable patch. I cannot recall any vegetables being planted in it at any point however.

As early summer arrived, Jamie was starting to toddle around. He was nearly a year old and could get around reasonably well on his little legs, more and more he

could be found clutching onto the wire fence for suppo
whilst 'helping' his dad in the garden. The only proble
we had was Bane – and I never thought I would s
that. Gary couldn't walk her any more without a b
ride and so she was not getting enough exercise for a b
young healthy dog. I would take her up the railway lir
when I got home, but I really wanted to spend time wir
Jamie instead. She still spent a lot of her day standing o
the sofa in the front room looking out the window an
barking at anyone who went past. Being able to look ou
the window and see people was a novelty she had no
enjoyed in Herbert Street.

But the biggest problem we had was when she came
out into the back garden. The couple on one side of u
had two children, maybe 6 and 8, old enough to go ou
into the garden unsupervised. Bane decided from the
word go that her territory was wherever she could see
and due to the wire fences, this included both next door
gardens. She wasn't used to other people in her world and
whenever the neighbours or the children came out, she
would run at the fence and bark extremely aggressively.

The children were terrified, who wouldn't be by a
Doberman coming at them, all teeth and snarling? They
would run indoors; I was terrified she would jump the
wire fence which was only 3 feet high. She could have
done so easily, although luckily it didn't occur to her.
And so, because I was afraid of her savaging next doors
children, she couldn't go out in the garden at all unless
I was sure they were indoors, and if they came outside,

we had to put her straight in the house. Very stressful.

I realised with a less than sinking heart that we couldn't keep her, it wasn't fair on such a big dog to get so little exercise and to be cooped up indoors all day. There was no big park like there had been at Herbert Street, the railway line did not offer her the chance to run around very much. Poor Vader was very much in my thoughts as I researched what to do, as I wanted to be absolutely certain that she would not get put down or go to be a guard dog either.

A call to the vets put me in contact with a charity that only took certain guard dog breeds – Dobermans, Rottweilers and German Shepherds. Dogs that would be often get picked up from dog rehoming centres via ruses of going to good homes and then live out their lives chained to kennels outside workshops or left to roam work sites and factories at night. This charity would spay her and if necessary keep her for the rest of her life but would try very hard to rehome her to a suitable owner.

I jumped at the chance to give her a better future and me less stress and I am afraid once she was signed over I didn't find out what happened to Bane, but I thought it was for the best and a better fate than Vader's, but yet again I failed to get the dog owner of the year prize that year either. Bravely, I did not consult John on Bane's fate as didn't think he would agree, so I went behind his back, but once he got over the shock of her departure, he realised it was one less thing for him to worry about and seemed happy with the outcome.

I know the neighbours were relieved as their children started to come out into the garden again. I did eventually become a successful dog owner in my 40s with a lovely cross breed rescue dog called Ben, not that this was much consolation for poor Bane or Vader at the time. And this is also when I found out that successful dog owners must face up to the fact that dogs have a tendency to eventually die on you and break your heart.

John felt that he needed something other than Jamie to keep him busy so said he was going to build an Aviary for small birds in the garden. I wasn't sure this was a good idea as these were going to be the small tropical birds that got imported into the country in their thousands at the time and due to issues of animal cruelty, thank goodness, this has all been banned now.

Love birds in particular were something he wanted. Yanked from their hot jungle homes, I thought surely it would be too cold for them outside, but he insisted, and they were to have an indoor bit of the aviary to get out of the cold in the winter. In order to build the aviary he chopped down the apple tree. I had not realised he was going to do this, and he did it whilst I was at work. The neighbours on both sides were rather upset, it was a very old apple tree, it had been there before the houses were even built, in the garden of the old house that had stood on the site. It produced hundreds of delicious eating apples each year that everyone in all three houses had enjoyed. Also, it had been the only tree in our garden.

John left the trunk and some bare branches that made up the centre piece of his aviary and it did start to grow again the following spring, but it was never going to be like it was. John enjoyed populating his aviary with about seven small brightly coloured birds, but they didn't do much for me, I think I would have preferred budgies, but they flitted about and twittered away.

Once the aviary was built and the birds installed, much like the pigeons he started to lose interest and in an unguarded moment one of the love birds escaped never to be seen again leaving the other one bereft without its mate. They just made me sad to see them as the winter arrived and they never left the shed bit of the aviary and one started to remove its feathers until it looked like a tiny plucked chicken. John's hobbies and animals always seemed to involve collateral damage of some sort.

Although being fair, his painting of lead soldiers hobby was fairly harmless to wildlife and he could quite literally do it for days on end. Painting model soldiers was for the most part done by grown men in those days, it morphed into a teenage past-time in the 90s with a shop called Wargames opening and selling cheaper plastic varieties of soldiers and also fantasy figures. In fact, fast forward a few years and Jamie was very into it as a teenager. John's armies were from the Napoleonic Wars, lots of horses as well as infantry. When painting, he would line them up on the dining room table and then set about painting a red dot on 100 of them before moving on to the blue braid and so on, each detail painstakingly applied with a brush made of a single hair, until all the figures were identically painted.

What was the point? I hear you ask, well they were ranked on shelves in our bedroom, and as such were something for John to look upon as something he had achieved. It kept him very busy for long periods, although I think this became more difficult when Jamie came along. It was probably quite therapeutic in its own way. The soldiers were purchased through specialist magazines with the sending of a cheque in a letter, and were not cheap, but I was happy if John was happy. It also led to a form of socialising as he started to go along to the local Wargaming society. I expect every town had one then, it was the equivalent of a modern computer gaming society.

Once a fortnight, he would meet with other like-minded men and play wargames. I would drop him off with his soldiers in their special carrying boxes (I think they may have actually been tool boxes), each man (I honestly never saw any female participants, but that is not to say they did not exist), would take out and arrange their battalions at each end of a very large table, and then using the throwing of dice and rulers and a set of very complicated rules, they would play out battle scenarios from their chosen part of history.

Some had WW1 or WW2 soldiers, others soldiers from the American Civil War, and all the way back to the War of the Roses. It took hours and John

..s fairly good at it. I would come back at the agreed
..ne only to have to sit and wait for the game to finish, I
..s told more than once that 'It's getting quite exciting,
..st the big final push'. But all I could see is grown men
..rowing dice, measuring and then pushing little lead
..ldiers about, and as I had to take Jamie with me it was
irly boring and tedious for us both.

In the end this hobby did result in us getting to
..cialise and have a bit of a life outside work and the
..ouse, although it was a bit short-lived as you will see.
he men that John was playing against had other hobbies
..f a mentally enhancing nature - they took part in pub
..uizzes. They were realising that John was a fount of
..nowledge, widely read and generally would be a bonus
..o the team. Despite it involving visits to the pub and
..drinking, I was pretty happy that he was getting out
the house and enjoying himself and before long, we
were getting the teenager next door to babysit and I was
going along to the pub quizzes too. Including wives and
girlfriends we ended up with 2 teams and could clean up
between us on a regular basis, my forte being geography,
biology and natural history of any sort.

A new board game came out about that time called
Trivial Pursuit, and the four couples involved in the
pub quizzes decided to extend the entertainment that
general knowledge could provide, and we started to have
Trivial Pursuit evenings around each other's houses once
a month. I quite enjoyed these evenings, as with the pub
quizzes they were the only social life I had. The game

with its pies or wedges and six categories of questions w
hard enough to be challenging and a game could take
evening, playing in pairs required agreement about t
answer which was often the tricky and contentious bi

For the first round of visits it was nuts and crisps an
bring a bottle, and then someone said that they wou
just cook a little chilli con carne to eat beforehand an
before I knew it, as the second round of houses starte
I had to cook a meal for eight people! This was stressfu
and suddenly it was not such fun. Delia was a help,
beef stroganoff with some rice served up to everyon
apart from John who didn't eat 'foreign muck'. Alon
with the hike in culinary expectations, the games got
little more serious too and a bit too competitive for me

We had started with two teams of men against two
teams of women and then as the women usually lost, we
decided to mix and match the couples with a man and a
women in each team, but not their partners. It could get
quite shouty and argumentative if people didn't agree on
the answer for their team. Finally, we got bored of all the
combinations and it was getting really late as the meals
were taking longer and longer we ended up playing in
teams of couples with our partners. For me this was not
a good scenario given how very competitive John was
and that we had both been drinking.

Once, we got a quite hard science question. I didn't
know the answer and neither did John, but it was my
'specialist' subject and as such I should have known the
answer, so I gave an educated guess. It was wrong. John

got nasty with me in front of the other couples, his voice dripped with sarcasm,

"My very intelligent southern posh wife doesn't know the answer, despite her science degree."

"My very intelligent southern posh wife turns out to be a thick as pig shit!"

"My very intelligent southern posh wife thinks she is better than all of us, don't you, darling?" The word 'darling', long and drawn out in a drawl of emphasis.

I saw the horrified expressions on the other couples' faces, John did not normally drip his vicious sarcasm in front of others, it was a turn up that's for sure.

"John, come on, no need for that," one of the husbands said bravely.

"You don't have to be married to the stupid bitch," he replied. "She thinks she is better than me because she works and all I do is look after a baby. You do, don't you, think you are better than me, than all of us?" His arms thrown out to encompass all of them.

His face was in mine, spittle spraying, his hand gripping my arm. I thought with horror that any minute now he was going to hit me, my shame was total and all encompassing. I struggled out of his grip and ran for the door, grabbing my coat on the way. Once out the door I just kept running. Over and over in my mind as I ran, I tried to work out what had just happened, what had caused John to flip in front of people we really didn't know that well. What was he thinking? Was this the end of our time of harmony?

I was consumed by worry and the possible ramifications of the evening. I had left my bag so had no money, so it was a long and cold walk home taking about an hour, during which I had a chance to consider if I would ever go back to play 'Triv' with these couples again. The answer was no. I cried and muttered to myself as I walked. I was seeing John's veneer dropping further and further, an escalation of his behaviour which up until this point had very clearly all been behind closed doors. He was home when I got back, having got a taxi, already in bed, the babysitter gone, my handbag on the hall table. I crept into bed next to him, holding my breath, but he just groaned and turned over. I wondered if he had driven past me in the taxi.

We never talked about it, but we were off the quiz teams and the Trivial Pursuit evenings. And even if we had wanted to, they just never contacted us again, and I was too ashamed to contact them, not friends then really, oh well.

CHAPTER SEVENTEEN

Finally, the Veil Lifts

All this time, our very lovely sunny little boy was growing up, walking and talking, always smiling. I wondered what he made of the noise that flared up occasionally. He was too small to understand, and he never cried. Outwardly, he seemed normal and happy. He was no longer a baby, he was a toddler. This was harder for John, as Jamie needed his time and attention. I suspect there were a lot of videos put on and still an afternoon nap. So perhaps I should not have been surprised at what happened next.

As I walked through the door from work one day, I could hear Jamie sobbing inconsolably upstairs in his cot. Not the angry cries he often gave if you didn't get him from his cot fast enough, but hiccuppy, tired crying.

I ran straight upstairs, he stood in his cot in one

corner, he was distraught, eyes red, "Mummy, Mummy!" he wailed at me as I picked him up. He was sodden, his nappy hanging heavy and smelly between his legs. He rested his head on my shoulder, "Mummy come, Mummy come," he said with obvious relief. I could hear the TV on downstairs, so I went downstairs to give John a brave massive piece of my mind.

Except it wasn't John on the sofa it was a strange man. I jumped out of my skin when I saw him, making Jamie start crying again. I soothed him with small rubs on his back while I whisper shouted under my breath between gritted teeth at the strange person on my sofa.

"Who the fuck are you? Where is John?!"

The man had stood up and was holding out his arms in a conciliatory fashion backing up as I advanced into the room.

"Babysitting!" he spluttered. "I am a mate of John's, he asked me, gave me £10, and told me to wait here till he got back."

"What about the baby? Did he tell you what to do with the baby?"

"He said he would stay asleep, he told me not to go in, to wait for him to get back, he said he would be back at 3, but that was 2 hours ago and he's not here, Look, no harm done, I'll go then." And skirting round me he headed into the hall and out of the door and he was gone.

I guessed as Jamie normally woke from his nap at about 3.30 that he had been crying for attention for

o hours. I held him on my lap for a long time until I
d to go and deal with the nappy, leaving him trotting
ound the living room with the air on his bare, very red
ttom.

I was still trying to process what John had done,
w did he think that this was a good thing to do? He
dn't know this man very well, that I was sure of, and I
dn't know him at all. He could have abducted Jamie,
r worse. I was appalled and very, very angry. I sat and
aited for John to come home. But when he did, he was
harming drunk, all smiles and big arm gestures and he
dn't really understand what the problem was, after all,
omeone has been with Jamie.

"Good bloke, Chris, give you his last quid, never hurt
amie, he needed the money, sort of helping him out,
ood bloke, ace bloke."

"John , you must never do that again, do you promise,
please, I am just going to worry all day every day at work
if you do things like this, please promise!"

"OK, promise, I will not do it again, but Chris is a
good bloke you know."

And so it went on, how could I have been worried when
such a paragon of humanity had been helicoptered in to
care for our son, and nothing bad had happened, had
it? I guess it depended whether you inhabited a child's
mind. They were given to trusting us completely 100%
to be there and we had not been, we had abandoned
him alone for what must have seemed a very long time
to him. Later on, he started to have night terrors, which

I suspect were linked but who can say how a toddle mind processes things? I realised that finally I was getti to the end of my very long, impossibly long tether, a that times they were a-changing.

As my marriage was unravelling, despite everythin there were normal and happy times and I think it important to remember this, as in part it explains wl the unravelling took so long. It also took so long dt to the ability I had and still have to compartmentalis things, to live very strongly in the moment, not to bea grudges and to easily forgive, whether this makes m stupid or a saint I will leave it to you to decide, but it a least explains my ability to persevere and endure. Anc so, inside this abusive relationship it allowed me to stil have happy memories.

I have a happy memory, although it is hard to grab hold of sometimes, it flits in and out of my mind, but it goes like this. It was early evening, I was home from work and had cooked our tea. It was late summer and the early evening sun was coming in through the patio doors into the kitchen diner. Jamie, about 15 months old, was in his highchair at the end of the table which John and I sat either side of. Jamie's highchair was a second hand one found by my mother, made of old fashioned wood, with a tray that pivoted up out of the way.

We were having fried egg, chips and baked beans with thick white sliced and buttered bread, one of John's all-time favourite teas. Not quite cordon bleu, but included all the food groups, so fair enough. We were eating off blue willow-patterned plates that my parents gave me with cutlery with red plastic handles to match the red and white kitchen. There was a strong smell of Sarson's Vinegar coming off the hot chips. We were all happy and smiling the three of us. John was recounting what Jamie had been up to and enjoyed that day. Jamie was sucking on a chip that had been cooled by me blowing on it while he reached out a chubby arm not wanting to wait for it to cool, smacking his lips and going 'Mum, mum, mum, mum', which wasn't my name but the noise that represented his subsequent sucking of the chip and so what he called chips.

These were proper 80s home cooked chips, peeled, cut and deep fat fried in lard in the chip pan on the cooker. The chips were delicious. I hate oven chips to this day with a passion, although I suspect there are a lot less house fires since chip pans went out of fashion. We used the soft white sliced bread to make chip butties with tomato ketchup, delicious.

It was a very mundane but happy memory as it was all so normal. Mum, Dad, baby, teatime; so I just wanted to write it down as I semi-remember it. I like to think it was followed by me bathing and putting Jamie to bed and then me and John consulting Ceefax which had replaced the Radio Times, to see what was on to watch, and then watching a TV programme. *Inspector Morse* started that year, so maybe it was that. John from his reclining armchair, me from the sofa, trying to decide who dun it, before going peacefully to bed. Those days existed, far more of them than the bad ones. I just don't remember them as they were unremarkable which gladdens me, particularly because of what happened next.

One Saturday lunchtime, John went out to the pub and he hadn't return by mid-afternoon so it was likely that he had followed the visit to the pub by a trip to the working men's club at the bottom of the hill. I had gone in there once having got home one day to find the house empty and making the same assumption, had gone to retrieve poor Jamie who had been in his pushchair in the smoky atmosphere for the whole afternoon, never mind in the care of a drunk father and his very dubious friends.

I was horrified, a snobbish southern reaction, by the lino, the sunken eyes of the drinkers, the thick cigarette smoke in the air, the overflowing ashtrays, the holes in the velvet seats. To my middle-class eyes, it was grim, very, very grim. Although, to be fair, Jamie seemed fine and he got a lot of attention from all the chaps in there, a mixture of older retired men and out of work men, they liked the novelty of a toddler, but the passive smoking was obviously not good for him.

Anyway, back to the Saturday night in question, it is hard to believe now in this ever-expanding digital age that you quite often had no way of contacting people who were physically elsewhere unless they were in their home. In order to get in touch, they had to ring you on whatever phone they happened to have access to, also, you as the receiver of the call, had to have access to a landline. The big wide world phone was usually a phone box or a public phone which most pubs and clubs had tucked away in a corner, or if you were lucky, out in the corridor on the way to the toilets. If you did choose to use them then this was usually only in extremis as they were very grubby unsanitary objects. And if it was in the body of the pub/club you always had to shout to make yourself heard above the general hubbub, not ideal at all. But John was not one to use the phone. Once he was out, he was out until he came back and that might be after a couple of hours or it might be after 12 hours. 11am opening to 11pm closing if the working men's club was brought into the equation, and 12 hours away from home spelt trouble.

This all happened not long after finding the strange man on my sofa, drinking events were getting closer and closer, closing in on me if you like. There was no time to calm down or recovery in-between, my stress levels were growing, sleepless nights becoming the norm. I was tired, I was still angry about the strange man and finally beginning to consider what options I had to bring my marriage to an end and eject John from our life without having to leave my home or end up in hospital. And so, when John had not returned by about 9pm, I decided to lock him out of the house. I had for once drunk a few glasses of wine myself and as such my powers of reasoning were slightly impaired. I will admit now that it was not the most sensible course of action. I had bathed and put Jamie to bed and then sat nervously on the edge of the sofa sipping my wine, muttering darkly to myself about how I just didn't deserve this.

Muttering to myself was a new thing, stress related, I think, and something I still do at low times. I had no real plan about what I would do, just wait for the knock on the door and what might ensue. But I was certain that I would not let him in when he was in a drunken state, as John being in a drunken state meant that I was therefore in danger. I assumed he would accept this state of affairs and find somewhere to go, except of course the flaw in all of this was that he didn't have anywhere else to go. He could sleep in the garage, I thought, the back door into the garage was open. Mind you, it was October and getting quite cold at night which under the circumstances proved not to work in my favour.

At about 11.20pm, John arrived back at the kitchen door which I normally left open when I went to bed, as he often failed to be able to use his keys in the front door as he was too drunk and then banged and banged until I got up to let him in. And so we had finally agreed that he didn't have to take his keys and I would leave the back kitchen door unlocked. Leaving it unlocked and risking intruders seemed easier somehow. He tried the door and failed to open it. He rattled the knob, he started to call my name, "let me in," it was not in an angry way, but in

ajoling, wheedling way, and this then became a sing
ngy way – "Ju-li- a," the note falling on the a, over
d over. The three syllables of my short name lengthen
t, I was finding this quite chilling, and also realised
at the neighbours were going to get involved soon if I
dn't do something. I approached the door and shouted
rough it.

"I am not letting you in! You are drunk again and I
n not letting you in! Go away, sleep in the garage!"

"Come on, Ju-li-a, let me it, its freezing out here,"
wheedling again, doorknob rattling again. Quickly
ollowed by "Fucking let me in you stupid bitch! Let
ne in or you are going to be very, very sorry!" He was
houting now.

The change from stumbling slightly hopeless drunk
o raging angry drunk was sudden. I now was certain
hat I must not let him in under any circumstances.

"I can't do that, I can't go on like this. Go away." I
shouted.

Carefully enunciated, word by slow word, "So it is
like that is it, well we will see, we will," and finally he
was gone. I heard the garage door opening and stupidly
assumed he had done as I had asked and would stay in
there. But no, he was back a few minutes later, a few
minutes in which I had stupidly just stood at the other
side of the door listening instead of acting, so I really
wasn't prepared for what happened next.

He had gone to the garage to get his machete, very
big and very sharp, the one that I wouldn't have in the

house and he had agreed to keep in the garage, but n
he was wielding it against the glass panel that form
the middle of the door. It broke immediately and
started to smash the broken pieces out the way. I s
stood stock still only a few feet back, too shocked
move. He smashed a hole big enough to get his he
through and then it got very surreal.

"Honey, I'm home," he shouted at me, grinnin
wildly, putting his face through and brandishing th
machete through the broken pane. You will need t
have seen the Stephen King film *The Shining* with Jac
Nicholson going slowly mad in a snow bound hous
with his family to realise quite how frightening this wa
Given that he also bore an uncanny resemblance to Jac
Nicholson only made it more chilling.

I had rather foolishly left the key in the lock on th
inside so he was now reaching through to open the door
Finally, I understood the danger I was in, he was going
to come into the house with a machete in his hand and
so I turned and ran to the only safety I could think off
– outside the house. As John finally came stumbling in
the back door, hollering 'Where are you?' in a menacing
way, I went out the front door fast. He shouted after me
"Don't leave, what about Jamie!" in the same sing song
voice as before. I ran anyway, I had to believe as much
as I believed in anything, that he would not harm Jamie.

Did I say it was cold that night? I think so, it was
cold and I had light clothing on and my slippers. I had
no keys for my car, no money and it was now nearly

nidnight. I ran anyway, away from the house down the road as fast as I could, thinking he might follow me. I ran to the end of the road where there was a local patch of grass with some swings. When I realised he was not coming after me I slowed to a walk and finding a bench in the small park, I sat on it.

An anxiety attack was upon me, I couldn't breathe, my throat felt completely closed, I was gasping for breath and also sobbing uncontrollably, not a good combo in the getting air into lungs stakes. I rocked back and forth trying to calm myself, trying to breathe slowly and deeply, get air into my lungs, all the while muttering out loud "It will be all right, he won't hurt Jamie, it will be all right, he won't hurt Jamie, it will be all right, he won't hurt Jamie."

A mantra I really wanted to believe, it allowed me to catch my breath and very slowly I got my breathing under control, my racing heart was slowing and the reality of my current situation was upon me. I was starting to shiver, but now I could not stop crying, great gulping ugly sobs wracked my body, I was broken by my life finally, there was no way out, no way anywhere, I was trapped and helpless, lost and cold, frightened and sad.

Everything that could possibly go wrong with my life had gone wrong with my life. I sat there for another 15 minutes. Thoughts went around and around in my head about what to do, muttering aloud continued, 'go to the phone box and phone the police, go to the phone box and phone the police' Now that would have been the sensible option. But you know me by now, I seem to inhabit a universe with different rules to all the sensible people, a world where keeping my life and pain private seemed more important than anything else, so no calling the police. I gathered myself to the point where I stopped muttering and stopped crying, and with the increasing shivering realised I needed to get back inside before I froze to death.

I had to go back to Jamie. I trudged back through the park and up the road, cold now in my bones. When I got back the front door was still ajar, but it was quiet inside, I crept in slowly trying to identify which room John was in. I heard him say in a tired sad voice,

"I am in here." 'Here' being the living room. "It is OK, I don't have the knife, I threw it out the back door when I realised what I had done."

I could hear the anger was gone, so bravely put my head around the door, feeling starting to return to my hands and feet, the tingling of blood returning really hurt, but absorbing what he had just said, panic suddenly rising, I turned and ran upstairs as quickly as cold legs would carry me, but Jamie was still fast asleep safe and sound in his cot. I went downstairs again more slowly and moved tentatively into the living room to stand in the middle, my arms crossed protectively across my body.

He looked sad again, "I would never hurt my son," he said, "Never! I am sorry for frightening you, I don't know what happens to me, I just lose it, but why would you lock me out the house?"

I looked him in the eye. "Because I am frightened of you when you are drunk and I can't go on like this anymore, I think I want a divorce and for you to leave."

I saw his drunk brain trying to figure out what I had just said. "I can't leave, I love you and Jamie, you are my life, this is my home, where would I go? I can't go back to my parents again."

John's narcissistic personality didn't really leave him with much compassion for other people, all he could hear in my words was how it would affect him, what it meant for him, he was getting slightly agitated, and I realised with my cold and tiredness I might have misjudged it again.

He patted the sofa, in that exaggerated drunk way he could have. "Come and sit with me, my wife," pause, "let's talk about it," he slurred at me, "Come!" It was a command, simple and direct. I did as his asked and moved to the sofa and sat next to him.

He turned to look at me, he did a thing he did, where he shrugged his shoulders, looked sad and then smiled in an encouraging way, this was all to make me think that all was well, and he was diffident and kind but after four years I knew different, I said nothing. He gently took my face in his and leant forward to kiss me, he got his lips to mine, but I was pushing him on the chest and saying "No." It was instinctive, not sensible, I was still very cold and my arms were not really doing what

I wanted.

His grip on my face got stronger and his lips were on mine and his tongue was in my mouth and then he was saying "Let's have a shag and forget all this silly business." He was manhandling me, pulling my bottoms down, they were loose, and it was easy. I was pushing his hands away every time they made contact, but he had his weight on me and despite being a similar size and weight to him, I could not get out from under him, but I kept struggling. He stopped suddenly and I realised that he was reaching for the large scissors left on the table next to the sofa (I had been sewing earlier, something for Jamie I think), the scissors were in his hand and there was a look of cunning and something else I had not seen, simmering anger, controlled though. The scissors were suddenly under my chin, the point pushing up into the soft flesh below my jaw, His tone had changed completely, it was cold and very angry, "We are going to fuck and you are going to stop making a fuss."

And with that the fight went out of me, self-preservation kicked in, self-esteem put aside, and so I stopped making a fuss and we did fuck, or more accurately he did. I didn't move, I stayed very still, he had put the scissors down and he took his shoes and trousers off and once he had started, I tuned out. It was mercifully quick, and so I just looked into the distance over his shoulder until with a grunt it was all over. Being forced by a man even if they are your husband is rape, in and simple, but in reality, I don't think either of us ... it that way at the time, I was being difficult, he was ...ing brutish, but not rape, definitely not.

From my perspective, he was scary and it was horrible, ...t I knew him and it was just more of John getting ...at John wanted and me being the brunt of it and ...ore importantly to me at the time, I was not physically ...rmed, no black eye, no broken nose, just my husband ...ho used to be called Dick, with a dick, being a dick.

He rolled off, got up and staggered off upstairs. I ...und myself pulling up my bottoms and sitting very ...ill. Despite the fact that he had not hurt me, I had a ...cream starting, and I stuffed my hand into my mouth ...o stop it and started to rock again, with a strange, ...uffled howling that came out in time to my rocking, ...t was coming through my fingers. I think that I might ...ave sat on that sofa for an hour or even more, more ...nane muttering "No more, no more, this will end, this will end." By the time I eventually went upstairs to the bed in the spare room, the night was becoming day and it seemed only minutes before I could hear Jamie chuckling and calling Mummy out to me, ready to start the day.

That morning, I knew with crystal clear clarity that my marriage was over. I had known it for a while really, but now that knowledge was cemented into my mind by the events of the night before. I would never live through another night like that, and that knowledge was going

171

to drive everything I did from this point on. I was go[ing] to get myself out of this and make me and Jamie s[afe] again, that I was certain of.

I started that day knowing that I no longer h[ad] feelings for John, he had managed to destroy them all [in] that one final act of drunken power and this had fre[ed] me to act and not be consumed with guilt about t[he] impact on him or Jamie, well in theory anyway. I a[m] also certain, that in the process of freeing myself fro[m] John, I was going to keep my house and somehow n[ot] have my life dismantled. John was going to leave th[e] house and never come back. It was a tall order, and apa[rt] from murdering him, I was not sure how to do it ye[t] but I was going to make it happen somehow and ver[y] soon. It gave me a small bounce to my step which thre[w] John and got me some strange looks when he finall[y] emerged on Sunday lunchtime. As usual, he said he wa[s] sorry, but I was not certain he remembered very much. [I] knew he didn't remember the scissors and the sex which had been a new move for him.

He looked at the kitchen door which I had taped some newspaper over. 'Did I do that?" he asked.

"Yes you did," I replied. "It was very frightening."

He apologised again. "I will fix it tomorrow when I can ring a glazier, leave it with me." But then remembering, he added, "You locked me out, you should not have locked me out, don't ever lock me out again!"

Still all about him then.

CHAPTER EIGHTEEN

Rock Bottom

The leaves were starting to turn on the trees in 1987 when we went down to see the in-laws the following weekend. Nancy was really not well, and I was starting to realise that she was probably going to die soon. I wondered how John would cope with that. She was in bed, but enjoyed having Jamie bounce around on the bed as she read one of his favourite books with him. I wondered if I could tell her what I was planning, but although I think she would have been on my side, John was still her only child and I didn't want to disturb the fragile peace she had with her condition and knowing she was going to die.

On the way home, disaster struck and the Hillman Avenger finally gave up the ghost with a leaking radiator and a subsequent blown gasket, and the repair costs were more than the car was worth. We found a house up the road to ring for the AA and so as we waited for the AA Man to recover the car and take it home, I realised that the first thing I had to sort out was getting a new car. John did not drive and did not have a mechanical bone in his body so that was all going to fall to me to sort out.

As the small amount of savings we had accumulated had been spent on moving to Crossfields we were going to have to get a bank loan. Buying a car was going to be no small feat; interest rates were climbing and I wasn't at all sure we could afford one, apart from the fact that I knew very little about buying a car, the Hillman had proved that. I would need a car very quickly in order to get to work easily every day and to get down to my parents. I spent a week walking down the hill, getting a bus and then walking up another hill at the other end, the journey took about 40 minutes instead of the usual 10 and was an additional drain on my energy and will. Another bus into town at lunchtime to see the bank manager, he agreed a three-year loan of £750. It was going to be hard to include the extra £30 a month payment into our monthly budget, but we needed to do it.

I visited the second-hand car dealers down the road and managed to buy a six year old Ford Cortina Crusader, trading in the Hillman in part exchange, they even said they would come and pick it up which was just as well. The Crusader was the top of the Cortina range, it was bright red with beige vinyl upholstery and a walnut dash, had a two litre engine and felt like driving a limousine after the Hillman. Despite the financial aspects of it all, it was roomy, comfortable and safe and I was very happy with it. Buying a car was such a normal thing to do under the circumstances, and of course, I didn't think for one minute about the financial implications if I did manage to get John to leave. That was very dim of me, although some might have considered the timing as good, as later without his income to take into account the bank would not have lent me the money in the first place, which also came back to haunt me.

Despite the ups and downs of my home life, I had been doing very well at work and really enjoyed going in and doing my job. It involved using my brain, being creative, meeting like-minded people. The environment was nice, the people friendly, and as I was pretty good at it, it was looking as if I might be asked to become a team leader as someone was retiring. It would only be as a temporary stand in to start with while they advertised the job. However, I was told that if I did a good job as a temporary team leader and applied for the job, my chances of getting the role full-time were good. This would result in a promotion to Higher Executive Officer. I didn't mind the extra responsibility and it would mean a pay rise, all good really. Also, with my quite short time there it was a real compliment, they obviously rated me, which really boosted my confidence!

This really was a Door A moment, but Door B was

slowly creaking open, and out of the corner of my eye, I thought I caught a glimpse of a black ear with a white spot on it, a mere hint of a whisker too. All of the stuff with John going on and the incident of the back door and the scissors were making inroads into my mental health. I had been brought up not to buckle, to grit my teeth and carry on, stiff upper lip and all of that, and I was determined that I would never be hormonal or emotional to the point of collapse. I saw it as a weakness I simply could not afford if I wanted to look after Jamie. Never mind expending energy thinking of a plan to get John to exit left, I was permanently worried about Jamie, thinking he was at home with a stranger on the sofa, or in his pushchair in some smoky club, or just being ignored by his father. He was at that age where he needed stimulation and to meet other children, and that was just not happening.

John was not going to take him to the park or to a mother and toddler group. The name said it as far as he was concerned, it was for mothers, not fathers, and I couldn't go as these events did not take place on a weekend, working mothers were more of a rarity in the 80s and the world not set up so well for them. Although it is more common now, babies being looked after at home by their fathers was not a very common thing in the 80s and there was no network of support for John. Being fair, this was not his fault, but it made me realise that we needed to fix it.

Also, if my plan to remove John from my life was

work, I would need to find childcare for Jamie first, particularly in light of the episode of the stranger on the sofa, which had not been repeated as far as I knew, but I thought that it was only a matter of time. I started to look for a local child minder as this seemed to be to be the least change for Jamie, swapping one home for another and after a short time looking, I found a lovely lady called Jan who lived on the housing estate that surrounded our offices. She had a couple of other young children in her care under five, she said she preferred the little ones.

Jamie liked her immediately and started going to her two days a week, it was expensive, money we didn't really have, especially with the new car and Christmas coming, so we had to tighten our belts even more, but I figured that the promotion when it came would sort out the short fall. It meant I had to drive Jamie there on my way to work and pick him up again at the end of the day, but at least I knew that Jamie was getting to interact with other children, learn to share and see what life was like outside the four walls of our house. He was learning to say words like 'book' with a very strong north east accent and two syllables, which was the word 'Boo' (as in say boo to a goose) followed by a hard 'k' sound, which sounded really strange to me although I tried hard not to be all southern and upset about it.

On his days off from childcare, John was going to the pub or down the club, making him even more unreliable. Despite having Jan, I found myself more and more

stressed by my situation, still unable to sleep, crying
the drop of a hat, and not being able to concentrate
work. So much for a stiff upper lip.

I made a doctor's appointment and managed to s
out all of my symptoms as the doctor handed me tiss
after tissue. With some gentle questioning he got out
me the issues with my domestic arrangements apart fro
the violence, shame prevented me sharing that, althoug
I think he might had read between the lines a little. B
the worries about the childcare were enough I think. H
said he would try me on anti-depressants, these wei
not the sophisticated anti-depressants of today, this wa
Librium, a blunt instrument in the depression stakes. I
had sedative like qualities and I realised after taking i
for a few days that it more or less rendered me unable t
do my job, or anything much else, although the sleepin;
was sorted. I was not hugely worried about John while
was taking it, I was not worried about anything!

After a few days, I realised that I could not have the
responsibility of a child and take this drug and so would
just have to stop taking it and accept the anxiety and
insomnia whilst working though my next steps. I also
realised that I couldn't take on any more responsibility
at work as I had no idea what was going to happen in
my life and didn't want to let anyone down. I told my
boss that I could not take on the temporary team leader
role. He was a bit confused but said it was my decision
and he was sorry it was not the right time. And so Door
A slowly closed and Door B cranked open just a little bit

more. Not this time, I thought to myself, I am going to sort this out somehow.

A chink of light appeared. One of the things that Gary had begun to do when he had moved out was train to become a Samaritan. He was good at it and he helped a lot of people to keep living. I think that the Samaritans had helped him when he was in Hull and having all of his issues around access to his little boy. These issues had never been resolved and he still had not seen his little boy three years later, which was heart breaking for him I know.

He now did a few night shifts at the Samaritans every week, on the end of the phone talking to the lost, the lonely and the suicidal and trying to help them. It was admirable and he spoke a lot about his work and how they helped people to find a way forward. It was with this in mind that one very late night, when John had just pulled me around the bedroom by my hair and the neighbours had banged on the wall and the man had shouted through that John should pack it in or he was calling the police; John did pack it in, then I waited for him to go to sleep and then went downstairs and called them.

I spoke to a nice woman at the Samaritans, standing in the cold hall as she listened as I sobbed down the phone, telling her what I was enduring and how I needed to end my marriage but wasn't sure how to. Once I had calmed down and she understood that I was not suicidal, but very stressed and trapped, she got me to talk about options. With someone listening i didn't seem to be impossible, she impressed on me that I needed to get either myself or John out of the house soon before something worse happened. She suggested I make some preparations just in case, not something that I considered up until then.

We discussed packing a bag with some basics for John, toiletries and clothes, and also a separate one of mine and Jamie's stuff and put them under the spare bed, so either set was ready for when the right moment came depending on how it played out. I thought it made sense, although I had no idea when that moment would come or how I would make it work, or whether it would be me or John leaving.

As we talked, we also agreed that it would be a good idea to buy a one-way open train ticket to Hull, which seemed the likely place for John to go if he left as that was where his friends were. If I could get John to the station and on a train with his bag, given his aversion to travel, it was likely that he would not be able to find his way back again. Easy. I got off the phone feeling hopeful and determined.

CHAPTER NINETEEN

Bye Bye, Daddy

Making plans for getting John out of the house made me finally realise that my idea that John could be redeemed and changed, and that somehow I was the person who could do it, had burned on the pyre of the experiences of the last month. There was no future with John. The realisation that I had to remove him from our lives, no matter what, was a moment of clarity that settled me and gave me a little peace while I waited for the right time. The opportunity arrived sooner than I thought it would.

One week later, I came home with Jamie who had been at his childminder all day, he was tired and sleepy but happy, so I took him into the living room and tucked him up in the corner of the sofa with a Thomas the Tank Engine video on quietly. I assumed John was out as it was one of his days off from child caring duties, the house was quiet, so I headed into the kitchen diner to start tea. I jumped out my skin when I found John sitting silently in the dark in the armchair we had in there. I could tell straight away just by his silhouette, the tilt of his head that he was drunk, but switching on the light revealed that he was what I described as gentle sad drunk. He had a several drunk personas, but this one was always the easiest to handle and always my preference.

I had a preference about my husband's drunk personas? Yes, I was an expert. I could rank them from 1-5 based upon impact, duration, ease of handling him, and risk of violence. We were strongly in 1 with 'gentle and sad'. He was full of melancholy and pathos, his words were slow and heavy, full of import, slightly slurred, his intellect still engaged,

"I am so sorry!" he slurred. "This is all so bad, I don't know how to change, but I will try, I will, really, it is going to be OK." So he had finally realised that I had given up, that I no longer cared. For a narcissist, that was a world class effort.

Poignant silence while I waited without replying, his head raised slowly, he looked up at me from underneath his too long hair, with his puppy dog look. "I love you. I love you so much," he implored. "I am a worthless piece of shit, how can I do this to you?" He hit the arm of the chair for emphasis about how angry with himself he was. He didn't want an answer from me, he was in full

w. "I wish you wouldn't upset me!"

The last was classic, even within the recognition and
e sadness there was narcissistic justification, off the
ok reasoning. I ignored it, still saying nothing, there
is literally nothing to say. Letting him ramble, my
ind whirred. He was never violent when he was like
is and was generally compliant to instruction, going
bed or eating if instructed, so as I sat and listened to
m rambling on with his sad and sorry thoughts, I was
inking, it is now or never. I had memorised the train
mes for Hull and I had a chance.

John loved a drama at any time, but particularly
hen he was sad drunk, so I think I was just playing on
is sense of drama, and his sadness. He leant right into
: and went along with it, like a script from a soap opera.

Finally, I found the strength to reply. "John, you
re right, this can't go on anymore, for my sake and
or Jamie's sake, you know you have to leave." I made
t sound as if it was his idea and amazingly he didn't
disagree.

"It's probably for the best," he agreed, arms now
wrapped around his ribs he rocked a little and made a
groaning noise. "But where would I go, to Gary's?" he
said hopefully,

"No, John, not Darlington," I said gently, reasonably,
praying to all the Gods I didn't believe in. "You need to
go back to Hull." Saying it to him, it didn't sound as it
if made any sense, he had nowhere in Hull to go, but he
had to go further than Darlington and I had figured in

183

my planning that he would end up at Paul's place if
went to Hull so I added, "You could stay with Paul
a while."

"Yes, he would have me," he agreed.

"Yes, you could get your own place quite quick
I would bring Jamie down to see you." I was sayi.
anything now to get him to agree.

"Would you, would you? That would be nice." H
was so sad, I was wavering. So I remembered the co
bench in the park, I remembered the scissors, and
found resolve. "Yes of course, he is your son, you wou.
want to see him wouldn't you?"

"Yes, yes, when will you come?"

"In two weeks' time?" I suggested.

"OK, but how will I get to Hull, will you drive me
We can go in the morning."

I knew that in the morning everything would be
different, all forgotten, it had to be now.

"No, John, its best if you to go now, this evening, I
have to work tomorrow, I can drive you to the station
get a train. Shall we get ready and go, have you got your
coat? I have some cash you can have."

It suddenly seemed very easy, he was completely
compliant, getting up and fetching his coat and putting
it on, his drunk brain functioning very slowly, looking
around as if he had forgotten something and pat searching
his pockets for his cigarettes and lighter. He leant with
one arm out on the hall wall for support, gazing down
at the carpet. As he was doing that I went upstairs and

brought down the small case I had packed last week and put it into the car. It had been hard knowing what to pack into it, but most of every type of clothing, and some new toiletries that I had bought, I figured it only had to last until I got his stuff to him.

John didn't seem to notice me putting the case in the car, he was deeply into his drama, the one where he left his family for their good not his. Getting Jamie into the car was a different matter, he had just got home and did not really want to go anywhere. He went rigid as I tried to put on the coat I had just taken off, but I produced a biscuit for the car and let him have his sippy cup with some juice, promised real Thomas trains and he was then happy enough to have his coat popped on so I could put him into the car too with his pushchair in the boot.

John was still standing in the hall looking bewildered gazing about, touching things, I realised the drama he was inhabiting, I could see it for what it was now, an extension of his narcissism, his absorption in only his own experiences, he was fully committed. I was incredibly relieved, not really believing it was going so easily. I spotted his house keys on the hall table and quickly picked them up and popped them into my pocket. Suddenly Jamie was in his car seat and John was in the car next to me and we were driving to the station. The train ticket and cash were in my pocket. I don't remember that car journey, but I imagine it was made in total silence.

At the station, I found a parking space, got Jamie into his pushchair and we all walked together into the station concourse, a happy family going on an outing. The irony of that was not lost on me, we had gone on maybe two outings in our whole relationship and they had always included other people. We had gone to Whitby with my parents in the summer only three months before, it had been a freezing day, Jamie bundled up in his push chair.

I bought a platform ticket for myself, and we walked out to the southbound platform. The train was due in ten minutes, it was going to be a very long ten minutes, but John bravely kept playing his part.

He hugged me tight, resting his head on my shoulder, mumbling he loved me. He hunkered down and held Jamie's hand, still lost in his own dramatisation, not yet recognising that it was real. Jamie said 'Daddy, Train', 'Daddy, Train', over and over.

As the train came into the station he got up and reached out and took my hand, I found I was crying.

"Do I really have to go?" he asked me, "I love you."

I let go of his hand, tucking mine into my pockets and taking out the train ticket and the cash. "Yes, you do" I replied, and I put them into his hand.

And he did, just like that. He picked up his case and got on the train. He played his part admirably, he stood at the window as it pulled out the station, one hand raised in farewell, Jamie was waving back. I found myself raising my hand as the train left and he was gone. I was crying more strongly now, not quite believing what had happened, Jamie was looking at me quizzically, "Mummy sad."

It was my turn to hunker down and look into his little face "Yes darling, Mummy's sad. Let's go home for tea shall we?"

It sounds surreal, but that is exactly how it happened, I drove John to the station, I put him on a train and Jamie and I went home and had fish fingers for tea followed by strawberry Angel Delight, our favourite. I cried on and off for the rest of the evening, tears running down my face as I bathed and put Jamie to bed, holding it together for a short Mr Men story. Mr Tickle was one of the favourites.

They might have been tears of relief, but John had been in my life for five years, he was the father of my very loved son and I knew that despite everything I was going to miss him, well the good version of him anyway.

CHAPTER TWENTY

It's Not Over Until it's Over

then finally allowed myself to fall apart and have mini breakdown (am I not the mistress of the understatement?). I allowed myself two weeks off work with stress. All I managed to do in these two weeks was get up, look after Jamie and go back to bed. I was so scared of John coming back and re-enacting *The Shining* that I didn't sleep well and jumped at every noise. Locking the doors even during the day, jumpy as a cat on the proverbial hot tin roof.

My nerves were shredded with good reason. I smoked a lot more than my 4 or 5 cigarettes a day, although unlike John, I had bowed to the new messages on secondary smoking and went outside to have them. I also started to have a little glass of white wine in the evening in front of the TV, it soothed me and helped

me sleep and I didn't have to worry about John see
it, or it triggering him to go off down the pub. W
hindsight, this is a habit that has not served me well o
the years (another understatement). For me, alcohol
an emotional crutch was a dangerous thing as eventua
I forgot how to walk on my own two legs without
something John had found out a long time before me.
was ironic that I found myself heading down the san
road.

For the next two weeks John rang me every nigh
often very late, often more than once, threatening t
kill himself, to throw himself of the Humber bridg
threatening to come up on the train and kill me. I wa
resolute, I was never going to have him back, it wa
unequivocally over. I said it to him on the phone ove
and over. "No! It's over. You can't come back." "Kil
yourself then, I just don't care, If you come anywher
near us, I will call 999."

I needed to be hard, to make him understand. I
was cold, never crying, never bending. I imagined my
tiger had stepped out from behind Door B, my friend
now, standing strong beside me (yes that one that kept
trying to maul me was finally on my side), deep throaty
purring vibrating through my leg as he leaned against it.
I thought about unplugging the phone, but the phone
calls also reassured me that John was still in Hull and
also I might need to phone 999 in a hurry if John did
manage to find his way back to Darlington. But as Paul

had taken him in as I had hoped, I thought this unlikely. Yes, he got angry on those calls, but I remembered he was 100 miles away and so managed to remain calm, as he screamed down the phone at me.

"It is my house too, and you have no right to throw me out, I am coming up there and I am going to make sure that I never have to leave again."

"No, you are not, John, I will call the police straight away, you are not coming back," I would say bravely back.

Jamie missed his Daddy and played up a lot, which given that John had been his main carer was to be expected. Daily tantrums when things were not going his way, being very clingy, his routine was destroyed. Once I emerged from my two week collapse he started going to Jan's every day and we just had to get through it and out the other side. My optimistic person buried somewhere deep inside started to come out again. Christmas was not far away, Jamie and I would have a great time, go down to my parents, but also have a tree and presents at Crossfields.

It was our first Christmas in the house, and we were destined to spend it on our own. I started to plan for the new normal, but I was struggling in all sorts of ways, financially, practically and I still missed John too which I had not expected. He had been a constant for the last five years, when things had been good I had loved being with him. My short memory, my forgiving nature, my low self-esteem, all these character traits of mine had kept us going. With his big personality gone it left a big hole. His things were all around me and I started to box them up so he could collect them. This is what had to be done to try to draw everything to a close

Of course he was right, it was his house too and that was something that was going to be tricky. Getting a divorce, getting the house signed over to me and John off the mortgage, all the while having to continue to communicate with John to achieve this. But for now, I didn't think about those things, I just tried to keep it together enough to look after Jamie day to day and keep John in Hull.

All through early December we had various versions of the same conversation over and over, pleading, shouting, crying, but he gradually calmed down and started to talk about getting his things, so we made some arrangements. Going back to work helped me to shift my focus, my work colleagues once they understood that my marriage had broken down were kind but didn't intrude. I didn't have a confidant apart from Gary who came over a lot and was helping me out, being kind and available if I needed anything doing and looking after Jamie if I needed him to.

John came back a week later to collect his belongings, in a van with one of his mates. He didn't have much to take, mostly his clothes and toiletries, his tools and his soldiers, and his many, many books, which I had boxed up to make it as quick as possible. I found it incredibly hard to see him, he made sad faces at me and tried to hug me and hold my hand, so I made my excuses, popped Jamie into his pushchair and went for a walk along the old railway while they packed the van. I then came back and made them tea and sandwiches before they left.

John was so obsessed with getting some sort of reconciliation out of me that he completely ignored Jamie, who had been so pleased to see him, lifting his arms up and saying, "Daddy home" over and over and asking for him to go and watch a video with him. It was heart breaking to see. I was the woman depriving him of his father, although in my heart I knew that it would be for the best for both of us in the end.

The visit and the van showed that finally John was giving in and realising that he was not coming back. As he climbed into the van to leave, I agreed that I would bring Jamie down to Hull to see him just after Christmas. His belongings were going into the mate's garage, as he was still at Paul's who was allowing him to stay for now.

He saw Jamie once after that in January 1988. I made the trip down to Hull and we all sat uncomfortably around in Paul's living room making small talk. John should have been playing and interacting with Jamie who was stood with his little hand on his knee just looking up at him, but he spent the time trying to get me to change my mind and let him come back.

When we finally got to discuss him seeing Jamie on a regular basis, he said he was not going to be able to move on if I kept bringing Jamie to see him. Even though I was sad, and I knew it was not what was best for Jamie, I had been prepared to keep seeing John on my terms for Jamie's sake. But honestly, I was relieved that it wasn't what he wanted and did not push it. He would not see Jamie, in the same way as he had not seen his little girl, the difference being that no form of maintenance was offered, and I realised that he was never going to help financially which was a blow, although I should have guessed that from the stopped standing order into the joint account. I could have pursued maintenance through the DSS but felt that it would be counterproductive to make him even poorer so decided I just had to go it alone. Jamie finally stopped saying "Where my Daddy?" when we got home in the evening and then our lives went in a slightly different direction, but for now we adjusted.

I had finally rung my parents and told them a sanitised version of what my life had been like for the last four years living with my very own Jekyll and Hyde. They were very non-plussed and couldn't really get their heads around it other than to say I should have told them, and they would have sent my brothers up to 'sort him out'. They were worried for me, particularly on the money front as now I was sending Jamie to Jan's five days a week, which was not something I had the funds for. When John had stopped his payments into the joint account straight away, I had been shocked when the money had not gone in at the first of December, this

been while he was still on the phone begging me
come back, so I was not sure what to make of it all.
w the hell was I going to manage? It made sense that
n needed his own money to live on now, but I had
t had time to think through the financial implications
him going, not that it would have changed my mind,
easoned with myself.

I had also told Don that I had thrown John out.
ancy was now quite poorly and I know it couldn't have
lped her to hear that news, but they needed to know.
on said that he knew it would happen. "Only a matter
time," were his wise words. He said that he washed
is hands of him and if he thought he was coming to
indersby to live with them, he could think again. So
oving and supportive as usual, what a lovely chap. I put
he phone down promising to bring Jamie to see them
ll the following month as normal (minus the pub visit,
hopefully).

Nancy made it into 1988 against the odds but by
February she was bedridden and finally taken to hospital
as she couldn't breathe without oxygen. I took Jamie
down to see her a couple of times between Christmas
and February and I think she was sad that she had not
seen John. I got the phone call in mid-March to say that
she had died. I let Don tell John via the contact details
he had. I was sad as she was really quite young, only just
60. Killed by her profession and a life of unkindness.
Her father George was outliving her too which was just
too unfair for him to bury his wife and his only daughter.

Strangely, given how badly Don had treated Na[n] on and off in her life, he was completely heartbrok[en] too. I guess he just had a strange way of showing lo[ve] just like John had. John went to the funeral, coming on the train from Hull and being collected by his fat[her] from North Allerton station. His first wife also ca[me] over from Lancaster to the funeral and I met her for t[he] first and last time. John was on his best behaviour; [he] had dug out his teaching suit and looked smart. He ha[d] a very bad case of the shakes, but insisted on flirting wi[th] both of his wives and trying to keep us entertained as w[e] sat either side of him in the pew in the church. It wa[s] a surreal experience and although I know it happene[d] I am not going to make up any more details as that [is] pretty much all I remember about it after all this time[.] After the funeral the three of us went our separate way[s] again.

The calls from John carried on sporadically for the nex[t] nine months, until I finally left Crossfields Road wher[e] I didn't give him my new phone number. I bravely gav[e] him my new address, so he could write if he wanted, although he never did. I knew by then that he woul[d] not have the means to travel anywhere far from Hull.

He had his own place within a month, just a bedsit, and he seemed to be managing and making ends meet, but he had gone back to his old friends, routines and haunts as if me and Jamie had never existed.

A quick phone call from Paul revealed that without

chool to keep him on the straight and narrow, he drank ll day and night and was physically in very bad shape, but I could not worry about that, he was just not my problem anymore, thank goodness.

Money was a massive issue. I had added up all my outgoings, mortgage, car loan and running costs, childminder, house bills, petrol and food. Nothing else, no clothes, no extras, and it came to more than I now earned including Child Allowance. I considered my options and rang the DSS, they sent me a form to fill out. I filled it out with all the information showing that I was in a minus situation.

They rang me back with their decision about two weeks later. 'You are not eligible for any sort of financial support,' they said. 'You have a well-paid job,' they said. 'It is not our problem that you can't afford your outgoings,' they said. 'You will have to sell the car,' they said. I think they may also have suggested I sell the house and move to a smaller one.

In truth, selling the house was a sensible idea in the long-term but not a very good short-term solution. Selling the car was not an option either, in order to work, I needed the car to get to the child minder and then to work, without my day being 10 hours long. If I continued to work I could earn at least 90% of what I needed, I was only 10% short, about £75 a month. The car was not essential, they said. They also said that I needed to get John to give me maintenance and I knew that that was the crux and not going to happen. That was

it, no further discussion. I asked if they would suppor
me 100% if I gave up work. Oh yes, no problem, we
will be happy to do that.

Brilliant! Well done, Mrs Thatcher, I thought, as a
single mother it is better to be jobless and live off the
state, then get a small amount of top up support to keep
working. Being jobless was not an option for me, so I
decided to go on the game... just kidding!

Instead, I spoke to my parents. I didn't want to take
their money and rely on them, I had a full-time job,
I had pride, but I also had a child to feed and a roof
to keep over our heads and so pride had to go out the
window. My family were brilliant. They rallied around
for a joint effort, and my parents and my three brothers
all agreed to give me £25 a month each, so I had the
£100 I needed to turn a minus into a tiny plus. I would
be able to feed us and pay the mortgage and bills and
the childminder.

My family continued to support us for over six
months, allowing me to keep my house, my car, my
job and my sanity. I have to admit that at the time I
also applied for a credit card, which as we all know is
never a good idea unless you can afford to pay it off,
but it bought me and Jamie that Christmas I wanted,
where I went into the House of Frazer and bought
really nice biscuits, chocolates and a Dundee cake and
a small fake white tree with built in lights on the end
of the branches, those being all the rage in 1987. I also
bought Jamie a Thomas the Tank engine train set with a

track in a figure of eight and three trains and a little Fat Controller (I don't think he is allowed to be called that anymore) which he absolutely loved. And the book; *The Tiger who came to Tea,* which became a firm favourite over the years. I do like a book about a nice tiger.

I am not sure there is much else to tell you that makes an interesting story. I spend the best part of 1988 living on the breadline with a good job, still keeping John at bay down the phone at regular intervals, sorting out getting his name off the mortgage, filing for divorce and getting sole custody of Jamie. And in the final part of 1988, I sold Crossfields and left Darlington for good for a new better paid job based in Staffordshire.

It was for a building society and came with a low interest mortgage as part of the package, which meant I could escape from the ever-increasing interest rates that the county was experiencing. It meant my family could stop supporting me and I got on with my life. I may have also had an unsuitable relationship with a much younger man for some of that time as well, but hell, I think I deserved it and it was lovely while it lasted. He made all that boring stuff I had to do a little bit easier.

EPILOGUE

So that's it, all done and dusted. Six years remembered and recounted. Someone who proofed it for me said 'It's a bit bleak!" Sorry if you have found it to be bleak too. It is dark and light, good and bad that makes up everyone's lives and it's all about balancing them. I had way too much of the dark back then, so maybe yes it was a bit bleak, but thank you for reading it anyway.

I don't know that my children will thank me for it, as you don't always want to know about your parents' life before you came along or when you were a baby, warts and all, particularly if there was blood and guts. But I do know I wish I had known more about my mother's younger life to explain her to me better, as it was, she remained an enigma to me until the day she died, and we were never close which I regret.

As to what has happened in the intervening 35

years, I am still standing and it's all normal stuff mos
Marriages (two more), children (two more), houses
more), dogs (2 more), cats (2). But here it is in pot
version in case you are wondering about both me a
John and Chris and Gary. If you not interested, y
could just leave it here and I won't mind in the least
my story is done.

The next time I saw Chris was in 1989, he had return
to the UK from Algeria and was working in the Midlan
not that far from where I was in Staffordshire then, :
I drove down to see him a couple of times. It was wei
that he had missed me being in Darlington, gettin
married, having a baby. We fell into our old routin
ended up in bed, which was lovely and nostalgic.]
made me think for a moment that maybe we coul
finally make something permanent work.

But Jamie was an issue for him. When I went to visi
Chris, he was single and finally free of Morgan, but m
having Jamie meant that our relationship was not going
to be rekindled in that way, particularly as he knew John.
He just didn't feel that it would work, he said he wasn't
step-dad material. I was sad about that, it would have
been nice and in some ways easy, but I got his point.
Also, I was still a bit all over the place and not ready
for another relationship, so we agreed to be friends, as
much as exes can be friends.

He met his future wife not long after that. I remember
him telling me on the phone that he had found the one.

tried to be happy for him, reader, really, I did! He was happily married for 30 years until his untimely death in 2019.

During the 90s and very early noughties we had met up about once a year if he was passing by my town for work, we would have a drink and catch up on each other's lives as best we could in a couple of hours. Over the years, I watched his hair go completely white in his 40s but otherwise he was exactly the same to me, still drinking too much, full of dreams and schemes to make money, memories stirred of a lovely boy in a bowler hat, a hot summer, a Dire Straits song, the drawings he did for me still in a folder in my study.

He stopped his passing visits in 2003 without explanation and I had not seen or spoken to him since then. I had tried to contact him on LinkedIn and the occasionally seeking text message over the intervening years, but he was always silent. I knew he was there, but that was how it was, and I learned to accept it and just miss him and wonder how he was doing. But in 2019 for some reason, perhaps because my own health was bad at the time, I was sad not knowing how he was, was worried he was ill too, so tried one more time to get in contact.

Facebook mining finally provided the answers and I found out that my fears were founded, and he had died only two weeks before at only 62 from liver cancer. I am not sure that my husband understood the tears, but I would have loved to have had one more conversation with Chris, to see his goofy lopsided grin across the table, to hear him call me Jules, which only he has ever done, that would have been lovely.

What little of John's life that I can tell you about is not happy reading. He stayed in Hull for a couple of years but then lost all his possessions in a fire, probably caused by a cigarette, I guess he was lucky not to have died. He did go back to live with his dad at some point. George had died and I think Don, despite saying he would never have him back, was lonely himself, but of course that didn't last long, the pair of them were far too alike.

Don died of lung cancer when Jamie was about nine, he had never been a very nice man so I can't say I was very sad, and this meant I no longer had to shlep up to Yorkshire to take Jamie to see him twice a year which I had promised John I would. Don left both Jamie and his half-sister his estate, cutting John out of the lot which must have smarted, although I was very pleased that Jamie finally had something from his father's side of the family.

John ended up in York at some point, sharing a house with another equally broken man and that is where I took Jamie to meet him when he was 17. John was then 56, but I was shocked by his appearance when we walked into the pub he had agreed to meet us at. He looked like a 70-year-old tramp, he had lost his teeth and his hair was greasy and long. His clothes were dirty and holed, all a result of long-term poverty and of course he was still an alcoholic. I think Jamie was both appalled and fascinated in equal measure and told me how John seemed to hold sway in the pub which is where the pair of them spent the majority of the weekend. He still had his charisma then and so he had plenty of hangers on. When we went back to pick up Jamie, John insisted on taking me aside and declaring undying love for me and asking if we could get back together. It was creepy and sad to see what had happened to him in the intervening 16 years since I had last seen him.

He and Jamie then corresponded briefly but then that stopped. He died before his 60th birthday of emphysema. He had me down as his next of kin, but I told the hospital I couldn't come when they rang, but his first wife went to hold his hand which was admirable of her. I didn't go to his funeral either.

When I try to make sense of my relationship with John, I think that my optimism made me believe that I could bring out the best in him, the qualities I admired, and that we would somehow live happily ever after. I thought I could bury his dark side in a blanket of love. I couldn't, although I tried very hard to do just that, particularly after Jamie arrived. Our son is the manifestation of that love, the legacy of something bad made good. To have Jamie I would do it all again, rather than wish him out of being.

I only saw Gary one more time, my family and I stopped off in Darlington on our way to Scotland in the mid-90s, it was nice but slightly weird to see him.

He was kind and interested in my new family, and fed and watered us on our long journey. I found out he had married the lady he had been seeing when I exited left and had a baby with her and now was divorced again. But this time he had custody of the little girl they had together, he seemed content. I was glad that he had not been separated from another child. He had worked hard and studied to be a social worker and now that is what he did, maybe trying to make sure that children did not lose touch with their fathers, to right the wrongs that he had experienced. I realised, a bit belatedly, what a good friend he had been to me during all those hard times, and I wish that while we had been in contact that I had taken the time to thank him for looking out for me.

As for me, I have lived through all of the years since 1988 as a flawed human being, desperately hurt by my experiences. It was a long time before I had any counselling and even then it was probably not enough. I had just packed it all away, gathered up my life and my child and got on with it, it was the only way I knew.

Luckily, I had the brains and the opportunities to do well-paid work and provide for us, particularly when it was just the two of us, as it was for a while. However, I continued to make my life mistakes, including ruining a perfectly good relationship with a very lovely man I had known on and off both at and since university. He came back into my life again after I left Darlington. He was happy to be with me and Jamie and wanted a proper

wn-up life with us, but with me not really in control
my faculties it didn't work out and I buggered it up.

This remains one of my biggest regrets. I think I
s still trying to find a way to be, but was still too
pulsive and continually searching for the next thing,
vas trying to find a way to be normal again without
owing how.

In 2002, I did a therapeutic group weekend with an
ganisation of women that helped me to release the
d patterns of behaviours and some of the hurt and
auma. The women I met on that weekend and since
ave proved to be some of the closest and supportive
lationships of my life, it was literally life-changing.
ou know who you are.

he rest went like this;

My third marriage lasted 10 years which was a miracle,
ve had two more children, a son and a daughter. I am
now on marriage number four. My husband Mike and
have been together 21 years now and married 16, he
s a very calm and quiet individual with a brain, a great
sense of humour and kind eyes, a good person to spend
my retirement with.

All three of my children are wonderful human beings
and I am immensely proud of them, especially as they all
come from broken homes. In Jamie's case, two broken
homes!

I ended up back in the south in a commuter town
outside the M25 where I bought my 4th house in 1990. I

lived in that house for 25 years including with husba[nd]
three and four. My second son and my daughter w[ere]
both born in that house. That stability for me and [my]
children was represented by that house and eventua[lly]
it made everything work out. I don't live in that ho[use]
anymore, but sometimes I miss what it gave me and [my]
variously shaped family more than I can say.

I carried on working in IT until I retired this year. [It]
continued to be well paid and interesting as IT evolve[d]
so I can't complain. I have always had a job, althoug[h]
I did do the stay-at-home mum thing for three who[le]
years in the late nineties and guess what? Earth mother
ain't and I proved to be pretty rubbish at it, so all pow[er]
to women who do choose to do that very valuable an[d]
hard job.

I have not been very lucky healthwise. I had bowe[l]
cancer when I was 47 and breast cancer 4 years ag[o]
at 59, both primary cancers and both noticed by m[e]
and caught early and treated successfully (so far, finger[s]
crossed). I now have heart failure caused by my chem[o]
drugs and this has also been treated successfully. I take [a]
lot of pills, but otherwise despite a physically damaged
heart I think that I am in reasonable shape for my age so
I have no reason to think my days are numbered.

Emotionally, I have often been in situations where I
cannot cope or assimilate things due to my experiences
which can be hard for others to understand without
the context. I have made mistakes by chasing love and
affirmation from men but not easily giving love back. I

have also been distant and unavailable to my children, too wrapped up in my adult life and my dramas. I love them all deeply and unreservedly, but I don't always know how to show it apart from with money and other practical things.

The legacy of violence can be hard to bear, it marks me out, it stalks me. I ran, I ducked and dived and then faced it head on. I had counselling, I started to heal, I tried to forgive, I forgot as much as I could and now as the time is right, I remember.

My life is still marked in ways hard to reconcile. My inability to deal with high emotion or upset affected my married life to my 3rd husband and was key to our breakup. I hate big sharp machete type knives and don't want them in the house – perfectly understandable really. I switch off Jeremy Vine on the radio if it gets too shouty when his callers start arguing. I can't watch any TV or films with sequences where people are trapped underwater. Maybe it is just jeopardy I have a problem with, having had too much of it in my own life, or maybe I have a mild form of PTSD? I still find it very hard to form good relationships with women, although thankfully with perseverance and not assuming that they always hate me, I do finally have some amazing female friends.

And still all the time I wonder if I am good enough. A good enough mother? A good enough wife? A good enough friend? And a good enough human?

I think I hold myself up to too high standards of existence, but that is also linked to what a failure I feel I have been over and over in my life. How could I have made so many mistakes? I have a strong desire to get life right now, having made such a hash of it. I want to walk through Door A with a cuddly rabbit behind it, to a life well lived and ignore the stripy fella I can see out of the corner of my eye, because I know he will always be there waiting to catch me out, to catch all of us out.

However, it is not his existence that I should worry about, but what I do when he inevitably appears. I would like to give him a big hug around his furry neck like the little girl in the *Tiger who came to Tea* and say "Bring it on, I can make this work." And finally, to answer my own questions, Yes, I am a good enough mother, wife, friend and human, and always have been.

I will not die an unlived life
I will not live in fear
of falling or catching fire.
I choose to inhabit my days,
to allow my living to open me,
to make me less afraid,
more accessible,
to loosen my heart
until it becomes a wing,
a torch, a promise.

Excerpt from a Poem by Dawna Markova,
"I will not die an unlived life."

ABOUT THE AUTHOR

Julia now lives in retirement with her husband and dog in south Herefordshire, within shouting distance of the beautiful Forest of Dean and the River Wye. She enjoys gardening her too-large garden, growing vegetables and trying to make it as wildlife friendly as possible. When not gardening, she enjoys walking in the forest with her Border Terrier Cross, Buster, doing jigsaws and cross-stitch and getting involved in village life.

Finishing her memoir has been the work of 20 years, and now it is done she really hopes that it might give hope to other women who are victims of domestic abuse.

RESOURCES

REFUGE
Support for Women and Children in the UK
refuge.org.uk

SAMARITANS
Suicide Helpline
samaritans.org

TOMMY'S
Baby loss support
tommys.org

DOGS TRUST FREEDOM PROJECT
Free and confidential temporary foster care for pets of
those fleeing domestic violence
www.dogstrust.org.uk/how-we-help/freedom-project

FURTHER RESOURCES
www.gov.uk/guidance/domestic-abuse-how-to-get-help

Printed in Great Britain
by Amazon